Create Any Life By

Thinking In
ONE Direction

What Most Teens and Young Adults Haven't Got a Clue About, But All Need to Know to Create a Wonderful Life

D1572207

TODD J. COURTNEY

Thinking In One Direction

Copyright © 2014 by Todd J. Courtney

ISBN   978-0-9903752-0-3 (paperback)
         978-0-9903752-1-0 (eBook)

Published by Teens Can Dream LLC

www.ThinkingInOneDirection.com
www.ToddJCourtney.com

Acknowledgements

Thank you to my young readers who provided valuable feedback on my earlier versions of this book:

Anastasia "Annie" Rousseau, Andrea Fernandez, Blaise DesChamps, Elizabeth Avila, Gilbert Avila, Jillian Duran, Morgan Wilson, Nathaniel Washington, Ovilee May, and Spencer Ryan. In addition, a deep gratitude goes to my own teens, Hunter Courtney, McKenzie Courtney, and Will Courtney who have read it more than most ever will.

A very big thank you goes to my nephew, John "Jack" Sieber, who was by far my harshest critic, but also provided me with some of the best advice which I feel made this a better book. In addition, a huge thanks to Andria Bengtson for her help on this book and the TeensCanDream.com stories.

I want to thank all of those in my business group classes, you know who you are, for continually coming back, and forcing me to be a better teacher, whereby I became a better student.

Thank you to the team at Jera Publishing for everything they have done to get this book to market: Ryan Evans for his editing; Stephanie Anderson for her design layout; Jason Orr for his book cover design; Kimberly Martin for her consulting.

A special thanks to my wife, Jacqueline "Jackie" Courtney, who has always been my biggest cheerleader and who shares my vision of helping the youth of this world.

Dedication

I dedicate this book to all the pre-teens, teens, and young adults out there who are interested in creating an incredible life for themselves. My gift to you is this book. Your gift back to me, and everyone you touch throughout your life, is what you do with the knowledge provided herein.

Help Stop Human Trafficking and Protect our Youth.
10% of all proceeds go to PolarisProject.Org

POLARIS PROJECT
FOR A WORLD WITHOUT SLAVERY

Foreword

AS A PARENT OF THREE TEENAGERS, seeking information to help my teens learn how to take control of their lives at an early age, I realized there aren't enough options for teens, and even young adults, to learn about the natural laws of life. I've read countless books in the categories of self-help, business and spiritual growth, and I realized there were a few common denominators. I also found that biblical text, as well as text from most all religions around the world, included the same common denominators. After realizing this, I had several questions: Why doesn't everyone know this? Why aren't we taught this as children or at least as teenagers? Why is it so hard to find this information? It dawned on me that the many authors around the world were really trying to answer those very questions. They too had figured it out and were trying to let the world in on this little secret. I truly feel they wanted everyone to know how to change their lives for the better. So they went about writing books to share with the world to do just that. In fact, I'm a fond reader of those books and have learned how to change my life in a very profound way as a result of reading them. But, of course, some of the books are better than others and some are much deeper than others, which could make it difficult if readers start off with a book that they don't understand, or a book that is too advanced for them. The result could therefore discourage young readers when it comes to learning, what Wallace D. Wattles calls, "thinking stuff."

My goal is to get this information into the minds of as many teenagers and young adults as possible. Do you want to be a starter on your high school team? Do you want a date for the prom? Do you want clear skin? Do you want better grades? Do you want to get into a Division I school? Do you want to be a doctor or maybe change career paths? What about owning your own home? How about making a positive impact on the world? Regardless of what your dream is, I can teach you how to turn that dream into a reality. So with the intent of trying to simplify my knowledge of this *thinking stuff*, to better suit the minds of our youth, I've written this book in a way that's engaging and relates to a broad audience of teens and young adults. Of course, keep in mind that I believe there are no short cuts in life; therefore, we should all continue a lifelong journey in the area of self-help so as to continuously learn how to better ourselves. Taking this into consideration, one should embark on reading the multitude of self-help books out there as there are so many good ones. I've also found, from talking with many others, that different books resonate differently with different people. What you like and recommend to a friend, your friend might just not like for his or her own reasons. With that said, it's best to read the work of many different authors so as to encounter different flavors and to read about the many different experiences each has had in his or her individual life.

Before we get started, I will tell you that my intent was to purposefully make this book short; I've found that in this day and age we don't have as many readers as there were in years past. It's not that people don't read. It's just that they don't read a lot because life seems to get in the way. That being the case, if it's choosing between two books, the majority seem to be partial to the shorter book. In addition, my goal is to attract a younger crowd with the hope of having enough impact to change their lives, given that they will eventually run our companies and our governments, and ultimately change the world. Since most people create things for others that they like themselves, then it makes sense that I would create something I might pick up if it were written by someone else. I hope you enjoy this compilation of ideas and philosophy to propel you, too, in continuing the lifelong journey of becoming a better you while learning how to focus your thoughts in one direction.

How to get the most out of this book

➤ Read it slowly and casually. Don't read as a novel.

➤ Complete the fill in sections as they come up.

➤ When finished, wait a couple weeks and read a second time using a highlighter on all pertinent areas.

➤ Go back to the book from time to time and go over your highlighted areas as well as all the quotes summarized in the back of the book.

➤ Familiarize yourself with the mind shift techniques and the affirmation in the back of the book.

CHAPTERS

CHAPTER 1

Utilizing **Imagination** to your advantage

IMAGINATION IS ONE OF THE most important of the common denominators because it is through your imagination that you create your world. Don't think about your world as the planet Earth, but rather the very personal world of *you*. You have your own mind, body, and spirit which constitute *your* world.

When we talk about the importance of imagination, think about it: You can't create anything without imagining it first. You can't move without imagining moving first. Where would you go? Why would you go there? What will you do there? What about picking up this book? How did you do that? Your arms didn't just randomly move and all of a sudden your fingers locked onto this book. Your eyes didn't just start reading the words on their own. Your fingers didn't just turn the page on their own. None of that could happen unless we had imagined it first. We imagine everything before we actually do anything. Before you start to study, you have to think about needing or wanting to study first. You're not just going to randomly pick up a chemistry book and start reading it. Firstly, you think of why you need to read that chemistry book. Before you go to a friend's house, you have to think about that friend first. Wouldn't it be strange if all of a sudden you appeared at your friend's house out of nowhere? Of course it would. But that's exactly what it would be like if you found yourself at your friend's house without having the thought first.

Be thankful for having an imagination because landing in different places randomly without warning would not be easy to live with. What about the simple task of taking your bike for a spin? Like everything else, you have to think about the bike before you could even jump on it and start pedaling. What about driving a car? Yep, same thing. Before driving the car, you have to think about driving the car first. Are you starting to get it yet? Virtually nothing happens without thought first. Of course, your heart beats, you breathe, and your bodily functions all happen, thankfully, without you having to think about it. But what we're talking about here is what's going on in your individual world. The fact of the matter is everything in our lives is created by our thoughts and the thoughts of others. Automobiles, houses, computers, phones, stores, clothing, were created from a thought first. How do you think Henry Ford started building cars? First, he imagined what they would look like and how they would work. How do you think Steve Jobs came up with revolutionary products like the Mac, iPhone, and iPad? He first imagined what they would do for people, how they would look, how they would feel, and how much they would weigh. The task of building them began only after they were imagined.

What most of us don't realize is that *all* of the good, fun, joy, excitement, etc., in our lives is created by *our* thoughts. I realize that many of you get this and it makes sense after reading it, but the fact is the vast majority of you haven't really spent much time thinking about it. You may be thinking, "Why do I need to think about it when I already get it?" If so, then keep reading. The reason it's important to truly understand that you, and only you, are in control of your happiness, fun, joy, and excitement is because the opposite is also true. That is, you, and only you, are in control of the thoughts that create the bad things, the negative outcomes, the angry moments, and sad times throughout your lives. Oh, don't worry. I know you don't do it on purpose. In fact, an argument could be made that it would be better if you did know you were doing it on purpose. Then you would know that you could change your life's outcome by changing your thoughts. But, unfortunately, the vast majority of people have no clue that they themselves, and only themselves, create their happiness as well as their sadness. If they did know, then the majority of people would be living much happier lives. Fortunately, you are young and blessed with learning this knowledge at such a young age. But, regardless of one's age, it's always a good idea to learn and experience the wonders of the mind.

> "Anyone who lives within
> their means suffers from
> a lack of imagination."
> ＊OSCAR WILDE

Let's break it down a bit more. There are really two types of thoughts: positive thoughts and negative thoughts. Positive thoughts are constructive in nature, and negative thoughts are destructive in nature. Think about this: Have you ever been happy and sad at the same time? I didn't think so, as it's rather impossible to be happy and sad at the same time. You have to be one or the other but not both. Our minds work in such a way that we are either in a positive state of mind or a negative state of mind. Strangely, the outside influences are not what make us either happy or sad. It's our thoughts that influence our emotions and perspectives. For example, you may see a car accident on the road and feel sad for those people involved. It didn't involve you in any way, but your thoughts directed you into a state of sadness. Or, if you're at a wedding and see how happy everyone is, your thoughts move toward a state of happiness for the newlyweds. In the end, how you choose to think is ultimately in your control.

If you asked yourself which emotion you would rather live with on a daily basis, your answer would be happy, and of course that would be the right answer. Who wouldn't want to be happy all the time? So, we have to ask ourselves, "Why am I not happy?" The answer is always the same no matter the context. You might think it's because someone yelled at you, which then made you defensive and made you turn to anger. Maybe it was because someone bumped into you, causing your drink to spill all over your clothes. Maybe it's because someone hit your car, or friends were gossiping behind your back. Maybe it was your best friend who's dating your ex. Do any of these sound familiar? Well, guess what? None of those are the answer. The answer is the same now as it has been since man started walking on this planet, and it is summed up in two words: *Your thoughts*. You see it's not the *incident* that makes us sad or angry; it's our *thinking* about the incident that makes us sad or angry. It's not the person hitting your car that created your anger—it was an accident. If you look up accident in the dictionary, you'll find it means "unintentional." It was your own thoughts that created the anger inside you. The person who bumped into you and caused your drink to spill *accidentally* bumped into you. You're the one who chose to get upset about it. As a result, you called him all sorts of names, and all he did is trip over something, which caused him to bump into you. The irony is you've tripped over things many times yourself. It's also not the person gossiping about you who created your anger. You should actually be flattered that people are taking their own personal time just to think and talk about you. And of course it's certainly not your best friend dating your ex that created your sadness. Heck, you broke up with her to begin with, and you told yourself that you wouldn't even dream of getting back together. So, what? No one else is allowed to date her now? You see, none of those so-called life incidences caused your anger. Nope. None of those. The answer lies within you.

You create the anger and the sadness because of the thoughts that go through your head right after those incidents happen. Those people did those physical things to you in your physical world, but you chose to think about it afterwards in your personal, mental world. You chose to run through the incident over and over again until it enraged you. You created the tension in your own body. Everyone around you noticed the anger in your body language alone. You chose to fire words back at those you felt had victimized you. You allowed this event, which only took seconds to happen in your physical world, to take hours, days, and sometimes weeks of your life so you could go over it time and time again. You chose to turn an otherwise happy day, or week, or even month, into one filled with rage and anger. You see, we all have been given the ability of controlling our own thoughts. Regardless of where you live in the world, there is one freedom everyone on the planet has, and that is freedom of thought.

We are the ones and the only ones who are in charge of how we think.

I was listening to an interview in which Tony Robbins was interviewing Dr. Wayne Dyer (both men are specialists in this thinking field) of controlling one's thoughts, and Dr. Dyer was using snake bites as an example. He was saying how no one ever died from a snake bike. It was the venom that killed them, not the actual snake bite. If we look at this metaphorically, the snake bite is what someone else physically did to you, but the venom is what you mentally did to yourself.

The next question is "Why?" "Why is it that I'm not happy all the time? If it's my thoughts that create my happiness, then I'll just create happy thoughts all the time." That would be nice, but the reality for most is that it's not as easy as it sounds. The idea of it is easy, but the reality is that our habits, upbringing, and society, have all had a hand in creating who we are and how we think about things. Unfortunately for most people, that's not such a good thing. All we have to do is take a simple test to see if the thinking habits that have been established are productive or destructive. The best part is the test is very simple. Ask yourself, "Am I predominately in a happy mood day in and day out, or do I allow people and circumstances around me to control my moods?" If I were to ask a group of people this question, most would actually answer that they are predominately happy. But when you start to peel through the outer layers, you find they really aren't living in a manner of a predominately happy person. The key here is to be honest with ourselves as we can't change unless we admit to ourselves that change needs to occur. Most aren't even aware of how they think and therefore aren't even aware that *they* have created the world in which they *don't* enjoy living.

For teens, it can appear even more difficult to be happy, as many teens are under the impression that being the same as everyone else is the smart place to be. Why is that? Well, for the most part, it's because teens are not comfortable in their own skin. They are not confident enough to be and do what it is they truly want to be and do. Therefore, many teens (a lot of adults, too, I might add) wander around trying to fit in by being like their peers. The irony is most of the teens they are trying to emulate are not confident either, so what we end up with are a lot of people trying to be like others who are just as confused as we are. Ultimately, we just want to feel comfortable being the person we truly want to be.

So, this brings me to the question, "How do we create the world we want to live in?" Keep in mind, when I say "create the world" I'm not talking about the world at large but rather your individual world—the one inside your head that you see, touch, hear, feel, and smell with. This is the most important world as it's the only one you have. The best part is no one else has a world like yours. Yours is uniquely you, and with the right kind of thinking habits, it can be the most incredible world one could dream of.

> "Imagination will often carry us to worlds that never were, but without it we go nowhere."
>
> ▸ CARL SAGAN

As I stated, your thoughts create your world. So, if you don't like your world, all you have to do is change your thoughts. For some, this won't be so hard, and for others it might be somewhat difficult. Start paying attention to how you think in your everyday life. How do you think about others? Your family, your friends, your teachers, your co-workers, your neighbors? What if your dad came home and gave a gift to your brother, but you didn't get one. What goes through your mind? Are you happy for him? Or do you feel a bit jealous? Maybe you are down-right angry you didn't get a gift. Now your mind starts playing tricks on you. You think your brother is your dad's favorite. You start thinking your dad loves your brother more. You create this whole made-up fantasy about how your dad doesn't love you and your brother is the favorite and it goes on and on. Not once do you stop to think correctly and pay attention. Never mind that your dad happened to be at a San Francisco Giants game, and because your brother loves baseball like no other person on the planet, he brought home an SF Giants shirt from the game for your brother. Keep in mind your father knows you hate baseball with as much passion as your brother loves baseball. But you never really stopped to think about the entire story, which was simply that your dad went to a game and thought your brother might like this shirt. You, being a science nut, might just get something when your dad goes on a trip and sees something that reminds him of you. The point of this story is that most people you know make up these fantasy stories in their heads. Sure, they'll come in all sorts of shapes and sizes, but at the core they will all be the same: made-up fantasies that sabotage your happiness.

Now, let's re-look at the story and learn from it. At this point, you know it's a made-up fantasy, but before you stopped to think about it, you turned yourself into an angry person with a lot of passionate jealousy. In your mind, the story became so real that you knew it was the truth. But whose truth? Of course, now you're looking at it with hindsight, but the key here is that you took a fantasy and turned it into truth within your own personal world. When you understand that fact, you can learn to use that exact recipe to create the type of world you actually do want to live in. In other words, if you create fantasies of how you want your life to be, and then believe with all your passion that you can create your new *truth*, then you will indeed create the world of your dreams. What is most important is you have to have the same passion of truth to create your dreams as you did when you believed your own story that made you angry. When you get yourself to a point of an unending passion of absolute truth regarding your fantasy, regardless of how far-out it may seem, your fantasy will eventually turn into reality.

This truth is one of the fundamental laws of the universe that too few people truly understand. But those who do understand know they can do anything and become anything they choose to dream about. How do you think Henry Ford created the Model T or Thomas Edison invented the light bulb? How did Colin Kaepernick take the San Francisco 49er's to the Super Bowl in his rookie year? What about the San Francisco Giants winning the World Series in 2010, when the critics called them a bunch of misfits? And then they did it again in 2012? Each and every one of them had a dream, and within that dream they created a passion so strong that eventually the fantasy turned into reality. The common factor among these four completely different stories is they all believed that their dream already was a reality. In other words, they believed so wholeheartedly that their dream was already a reality that it became a matter of "when" versus a matter of "if." In summary, they each focused their thoughts in one direction.

One might say this is very easy. "Sure, I can do that. How hard can it be to create dreams?" Well, the answer is not hard at all; it's quite easy to create a dream. The hard part is to believe in your dreams with unwavering confidence. A lot of this really depends on one's personality and how he or she was raised. I either read in a book or heard in a seminar that some psychologists believe that by the age of 13 we have already established roughly 90% of our habits, including our thinking. This means you need to become aware of your thoughts and your habitual thinking patterns. Ask yourself if you're happy in life. Ask yourself if you're able to achieve your goals. If you're like most people, the answer is "no." But, it's not due to the outside forces you've been thinking about. It's not because your dad lost his job. It's not because your parents fight all the time. It's not because people don't like you or because you have horrible teachers. It's not because of the neighborhood you live in or because of your boss at work. Sure, all of that can make it easier or more difficult, depending on your situation, but in the end it's all been because of *your* thinking habits.

> ## "Reality can be beaten with enough imagination."
> ### ‣ MARK TWAIN

One of the most important things to remember in life is that "likes attract likes," which is where the phrase "birds of a feather flock together" comes from. What this means is happy thoughts attract more happy thoughts. Of course, the opposite is also true, in that negative thoughts attract more negative thoughts. This is very, very important to pay attention to. The truth is most of us just emulate or copy how our parents, siblings, co-workers, and friends act because we think that's normal. Unfortunately, it is normal for them to be like that. But, just because it's *their* normal doesn't mean it's right. Think about the word 'normal.' All it means is that when something is done over and over again, the pattern becomes a normalized condition, and therefore many people think it must be okay to do. Let's go way back to the days of the Vikings. It was normal for them to kill women and children and burn villages. When we had slavery in this country, it was normal to own people as slaves and force them to work. Many of us who grow up in inner-city projects or affluent neighborhoods might see it as normal to deal and take drugs as well as steal from others to support drug habits. A major drawback of following or copying someone else's normal is that it could be destructive in nature, such as those examples from history, in which case you've just created a destructive habitual thinking pattern for yourself. Because this habit was destructive in nature, you've now put yourself in the position of creating a world for yourself that you won't want to live in.

Worse yet, without learning how to pay attention to ourselves and create the type of world we do want to live in, you just keep following the customs of those who came before us. Much of this most likely comes from your mother or your father or both. The sad truth of the matter is no one ever taught them how to think this way, and therefore all they knew was to copy others, such as your grandparents. But don't beat yourself up over it. In fact, don't beat them up over it either. People only know what they know, so it's unfair for you to judge them. You most likely didn't know this yourself until you picked up this book and started to read it. Just be glad you did, as happy thoughts will attract more happy thoughts.

Maybe someday you'll be able to show your parents and friends this book and the countless others out there on the subject of bettering ourselves. But, be cautious. Most people don't like to be told to change or that they need to change. In fact, that typically has the opposite effect. The best way is to show people through your own change. After you learn how to be a continuously happy person, your friends and family will take notice. People you don't know will also take notice. More people of a happy nature will be drawn to you because likes attract likes. As I mentioned earlier, "birds of a feather flock together." This is why you see pigeons flying with other pigeons and hawks with hawks. Eagles hang out with eagles, and doves stay with other doves. It's not that they can't or don't coexist with the other birds because they do. We've all seen many types of birds in the same area. But, they typically don't nest together because that is nature's way. Humans have the same sort of system, but it's limited only to the mind. As humans on this planet, we are all the same, and like minds tend to be drawn together. So, we all don't have to think in the same way to coexist. In fact, we wouldn't want to be the same. That would be like only having one type of bird or one type of tree or one type of animal. How boring would that be? We can all get along, especially if we train ourselves how to create our own individual happiness.

You might be wondering how imagination plays in all this. Well, think about it this way. Let's say you don't like the color of your room or apartment. Okay, paint it another color. But, you have to imagine the color you would like first. Or, what if you weren't enjoying the book you were reading? Well then, imagine what kind of book would interest you and go find it. Let's dig a bit deeper. What if a friend or co-worker of yours was getting on your nerves or putting you down in front of others, which made you very angry? I'm sure your normal response would be to think about how much you hated the person for doing that. You would probably talk to others about the situation and try to get them to dislike that person as well. Then you would text other people about that one person. Of course, when you get home and your family or roommate notices your anger at the dinner table, the conversation is all about this other person who did all this stuff to you. When you go to bed, you still feel so angry that you find it hard to fall asleep. All in all, that's about ten hours of your day, and most of the focus would be on this other person. Strangely enough, the other person wouldn't be thinking about you at all, but you would have spent the majority of your day allowing that person into your world. I used the word *allowing*, which means *you* chose to think about this person. Now, if you chose, then of course you had a *choice*. Of course, if you had a choice and chose the option to think about this person, then you had a choice not to. You see, we always have choices. Is it easy? Not always. But it's always a choice, and it's your choice.

STOP HERE

On the following lines, write down any negative situations that are occupying your mind right now and explain what you feel the issue is. After you finish, let it go. Now that you've acknowledged it, it will be easier to set yourself free of it.

Okay then. Let's get back to imagination. If something or someone is bothering and consuming your thoughts, you have to train yourself to get rid of those thoughts. We do this through imagination. The beautiful thing is that we can use our imagination to take us anywhere or think about anything. It's through imagination that every product ever made was created. It's using our imagination to create our travel plans for vacation. For those in school, it's through imagination that you determine what to do after school, or on weekends, and with whom you want to do those things. As you do this, you will forget the negative issue that was previously occupying your mind. Allow your imagination to take you anywhere and everywhere you want to go. Use it to create fantasies. How do you think movies are made? People just don't show up to the movie studios and start filming. A script has to be written first, and that writer uses his imagination to create every word and every scene. Sometimes, such as in science fiction movies like Avatar, the writer uses his imagination to the extreme and ends up creating something no one has ever thought of before. That's exactly what you want to do—go to the extreme. If you don't like the way you look, imagine hair changes, clothing changes, work out changes. Don't settle in a state of unhappiness.

If you don't have much money or maybe your family doesn't have much money, get out of that feeling. Use your imagination to think about what you would do if indeed you did have more money. Where would you go? Who would you take with you? Where would you live? What does the house look like? What kind of car do you drive? What color is the car? You see, change comes first from the imagination. If you can't imagine yourself looking better, having more money, having a nicer home, or having a nicer car, then how do you expect change to come to you? I'm here to tell you it won't. You'll stay in exactly the same manner you are now. Sure, some day you might have different clothes, a different car, and even a different home. But overall, your state of being will be the same.

STOP HERE

Write down what it is you want. It can be anything. Maybe it's something small you want now, or maybe it's a big dream you want in the future. It doesn't matter. The most important thing is to write it down.

_____

_____

_____

_____

_____

_____

_____

_____

"Disneyland will never be completed.
It will continue to grow as long as
there is imagination left in the world."
➤ WALT DISNEY COMPANY

Growing up in San Jose, California, I lived near an exclusive golf and country club. Some of the kids at school lived in that area, and a few were members of the club as well. I had always wished our family belonged, but the truth was my father didn't play golf, nor could we afford it. In high school, friends of mine worked at the club, and I got a job selling ice cream at one of the major golf tournaments. It was then that I decided someday I would live in that area and would join the club. Years later, after being married and my wife pregnant with twins, we decided we needed a larger home. We now have a nice home on that golf course and are members of the golf club. To clarify here, I was very interested in golf and wanted the convenience of being close to a course to play on. When I reflect back on those thoughts I had as a young teenager, I'm amazed at how things unfolded because at that time I had no idea how powerful imagination was.

We have to learn to use our imaginations to create better lives versus using them as most people do, which keeps us in the same individual world we don't like to live in. Albert Einstein said, "Imagination is more important than knowledge." Think about this for a moment. The same guy who said this is considered one of the greatest geniuses to walk the planet. Don't over think this. As Nike says, "Just do it." I realize this may sound foreign to many of you, but take a look in the mirror and ask yourself if you like living in your individual world. Well, if you don't—or don't like it the majority of the time—then you must change your way of thinking in your inner world before change occurs in your outer world. Albert Einstein also gave us the definition of insanity: "doing the same thing over and over again while expecting different results." This is where we need to be careful not to let our ego control the way we think, which only results in not changing our habitual thinking habits. Remember it is *your* thoughts—and *your* thoughts only—that can put an end to your unhappiness. Once you understand that, then and only then can you start the process of change to create the world you really want to live in.

Chapter Summary

➤ Nothing happens without imagining it first.

➤ All the joy, fun, and excitement in our lives is created by our thoughts. Of course, the opposite is also true.

➤ It's our thoughts that influence our emotions and perspectives.

➤ Most aren't even aware of how they think and therefore aren't even aware that they have created the world in which they don't enjoy living.

➤ If you don't like your world, all you have to do is change your thoughts.

➤ If you create fantasies of how you want your life to be, and then believe in them so as to create your new truth, then you will indeed create the world of your dreams.

➤ Roughly 90% of our habits are established by age 13.

➤ Birds of a feather flock together. Therefore, positive
  thoughts attract more positive thoughts.

➤ Allow your imagination to take you anywhere and
  everywhere you want to go.

➤ Remember that it is your thoughts and your thoughts
  only that can put an end to your unhappiness.

CHAPTER 2

Using **belief** to get what you want

WHEN IT COMES TO ALMOST anything, your belief and faith in yourself is a much larger part in making things happen in your individual world than most people think. In fact, most of us tend to sabotage what we want just because we really don't understand what belief is. Sure, we all know the basic definition of belief, such as I believe in God or I believe this or that to be true, but most of us don't know how to use faith to our advantage. Much like I presented in the first chapter on imagination, faith comes from a state of mind. Do you know the difference between faith and hope? Most of us sense the difference, but most are not able to articulate it well enough to understand precisely what each of the words truly mean. As you read this next chapter, you will not only understand the difference but you'll also be able to explain the difference to someone else.

So the question we tend to ask ourselves is "Why am I not getting what I want? I prayed for it so it should be here. I believed I was going to get it, but it's been a long time, and I still don't have it. I put pictures up on my wall and think about it all the time but still nothing." You start talking inside your head telling yourself that this thinking stuff doesn't work. "I did exactly what my mom and dad said to do, and nothing has come of it." Now you're thinking your mom and dad don't know what they're talking about. "Nope, Mom. Nope, Dad. This stuff doesn't work." You think that you're never going to get that new dress, good grades or new job. The list goes on and on, and although what is on the list is different for each of us (since we all have different desires), the results are the same. You're right! You're not getting what you want! You know why? Just think about what's been going on inside your head. Although you wanted something, or more than one thing, when you didn't get it in the time frame you wanted, *you* started to reverse course. *You* started changing the thoughts in your head, which of course pushed away the very things you said you wanted. Unfortunately, this behavior—or "habitual thinking habits," as I like to say—is followed by the masses, which means the majority of people think just like you. Oh, and just so you know, that's not a good thing. This is a time when you clearly want to be in the minority group, because it's this small group who knows how to attract what it is they want versus pushing away that which they want.

> **"Difficult takes a day, impossible takes a week."**
> **▸JAY Z**

Why is it only a small percentage of people know how to attract what they want? There are multiple reasons for this. Some had parents who figured it out and taught their children how to do the same. I think others instinctively are able to figure it out on their own, although that is a much smaller group of people. Still, some others have a sense to seek this information out on their own, but I think this is the smallest group of people. Regardless of the reason, the important fact to remember is anyone can learn and teach themselves how to create the world of their dreams. The fact that you're reading this right now shows that you too are a seeker and are looking for ways to enhance your life. I was a seeker, and the more I found and learned, the more I was driven to learn even more. It's as if some unseen force is pushing me to keep seeking.

It all started in 2006. My wife and I were at the San Francisco Airport on our way to Ixtapa, Mexico, to stay with some friends. While walking through the airport, my wife stopped at a book store to pick up some magazines as she normally does. There was a brand new book out, being displayed like most new books, called *The Secret* by Rhonda Byrne. My wife had heard about it from her sister, so she bought it, which then made me wonder what I would do for three hours when originally I thought I would be chatting with her. Normally we would not purchase two of the same books, but after she told me what she had heard about it, I had to have a copy. In fact, I couldn't wait to read the book. I was two thirds through it when we arrived in Ixtapa, and I was in complete amazement. I started to recall a flood of questions I had when I was a teenager, regarding life and the world. I'm sure the flight attendant thought I was a bit odd with my jaw dropped open while reading. We both finished the book during our stay, and in fact I kept re-reading it. At various times during the vacation, we would look at each other in amazement when we saw a situation unfold before us that was clearly created by that person's own thoughts. The most powerful and jolting was when two of the men staying with us got a little heated toward one another. One of them slammed the glass door to close the other out only to have the two-thousand-dollar door shatter into pieces. That's right! Two thousand dollars, not Mexican pesos, vanished in mere seconds because he wasn't in control of his thoughts. It was that one trip, that one stop in the airport bookstore, and that one book that propelled me on a path to learn as much as I could. I used this knowledge to better my relationship with my wife, my kids, my friends, and my clients. I became happier and freer in everyday life. I used this knowledge to virtually double the revenue in my business in five years, which originally took me twenty years to reach. I pushed myself to the top 2% in the company, and now I'm willing to give that up so I can focus on helping you, the teenager and young adult, create the life of your dreams.

At this point, it's truly a case in which I could never ever go back to the old me. Once you find something this powerful that works and changes your life in so many ways, going back to the old you would be insane. I promise you that if you too seek more and more information on how to create the life one dreams about, you will attract everything you've ever wanted. It truly is that easy but it takes practice. Think about sports for a moment. If you wanted to be a good baseball player, football player, soccer player, or basketball player, you'd have to practice. For those who understand this thinking stuff, not only do I mean practice in the physical sense, but also practice in the mental sense.

When I was coaching girls' softball, I would teach the girls how to think prior to their stepping up to the plate.

I wanted them to visualize seeing where the ball would go. Would it be a grounder or fly ball, and what base they would get to? To their surprise, this technique worked much of the time. During a championship game, my daughter was pitching. Because we were the underdogs, we had to beat the opposing team two out of three times to make the championship game. It was an incredibly hot day at 102 degrees. I explained to the girls that the team who focused on the game and not the heat would win. Sure enough, as I was first base coach during our offense, I could hear the complaints from the other dugout. I knew we were beating them mentally. But, they were tough competitors. What they also didn't know was that I had been teaching my daughter to visualize each pitch before she threw the ball. The opposing coach, known to be a bit of a hot head, was getting furious, thinking my daughter was trying to cause delays and catch the batter off guard. I'm sure you can guess which team became the league champions!

There are no short cuts in life, and although your life will be so much easier as you learn this *thinking stuff,* you will still be moved to take action towards your goal. But the beauty of understanding this is that as you take action it won't feel like "work" in the normal sense of the word because you'll know it's moving you towards your goal. Nonetheless, you will still be prompted to take action, because without any action on our part, we wouldn't appreciate what it is we want to the degree we should. If we just ask and are given everything we ask for, we would lose our zest for life. You may not realize it, but life would be very boring. Think about the toys you received for Christmas when you were younger. You just had to have them, until eventually the newness wore off and you stopped playing with them. That happens to most people, even with big toys, such as boats, motorcycles, jet skis, and the like. I know you say you would never get bored with them, but trust me, you would and you do.

Let's go back to sports for a minute. As I mentioned, you have to practice to become good. It's not like you could have a friend practice for you and then you show up to the game ready to play. But, because your personal goal was to become a better player, you no longer consider practicing as work or a chore. You enjoy the process because it's pushing you towards obtaining your personal goal of becoming a better player. The same idea goes for homework or tests. You can't have a friend study for you and then you take the test. Of course not; you would fail. Oh, that may sound like a good plan, but the reality is it won't work. Of course, common sense tells us that wouldn't work because it's an easy example. But this applies to anything we want out of life. If wanting a new job or a promotion is your desire, then you should master your current job and as others take notice, new opportunities will arise. If you want something bad enough and use this *thinking stuff* to achieve it, you will get little messages in your head, in the form of ideas, telling you what type of action you should take toward achieving that which you desire. If you want to go to college, or better yet know exactly which college you would like to go to, then *you*'ll get these messages on what you'll need to do in order to get into that college. If it's certain grades in certain classes, then these messages will probably tell you to study more or get into a study group. If it's a trade school, you will get messages in the form of ideas on what to do. Again, there are no shortcuts, and if you think it boils down to luck, guess again. Luck is what you make of it. As the saying goes, "the harder you work, the luckier you get." I would like to add something to that to enhance that phrase: "the harder you work and the smarter you think, the luckier you get." Now, don't confuse the term "hard work" with the conventional meaning. What I mean is you're going to have to work on learning this *thinking stuff*. As you do, you'll get those internal messages pushing you in the right direction towards your goal. If you choose not to listen and take action on those messages, then maybe you're not as truly dedicated to your goal as you once thought.

"The smarter you think"—what does that mean? Well, it doesn't mean being smart in an academic sense, although it helps. What it really means is thinking correctly. This goes back to what I was saying earlier on: belief and faith. Remember what I mentioned in the previous pages on how most people start changing their thought process when they don't get what they want in the timeframe in which they want it? Well, that's what

I would call an incorrect thinking habit. That's because they've trained themselves to reverse target when they don't get what they want when they want it. It's really not their fault because most people haven't been taught how to think correctly. I'm not talking about logical thinking here because like Albert Einstein said, "Logic will get you from A to B but imagination will take you anywhere." I'm talking about outside-of-the-box-thinking—thinking that is completely different from what you're used to. Hey, if you knew how to think correctly, you wouldn't need to read this book. I'm talking about learning how to use your imagination to think about what you want and then using faith to *know* you'll get it. I use the word *know* because it's the key to faith. By that I mean having faith and truly having faith, knowing without any wavering doubt that you will have that which you desire.

But, now we have to take it a step further. Not only do you have to know you'll have it, you actually have to believe you are already in possession of what you want. I know it sounds confusing, especially since for most of you this is the first time you've ever heard of this concept. But, all I can tell you is that's how it's done. You see, without believing you already have that which you desire, you are doing the opposite: believing you don't. So, if you believe you don't have it, then of course you most likely will not get it because your thoughts of not having it keep pushing it farther and farther away. Many of you have probably read or heard the phrase, "Ask and ye shall receive." It doesn't say, "Ask a thousand times and you might get it." It says "ask" in the singular. The fact is, if you keep asking over and over again, it means you don't believe you have it. Therefore, because you believe you don't have it, you don't get it. I know this may be a bit confusing, so you may want to re-read this section until you understand it completely.

> *"Faith is taking the first step when you don't see the whole staircase."*
> ➤ *MARTIN LUTHER KING, JR.*

One may ask, and it would be quite normal to ask, "How am I supposed to believe I have something when in fact I don't have it? That doesn't make any sense to me." I realize it doesn't make sense to you, but keep in mind the reason it doesn't make any sense to you is because you've never been told this or taught this information before. If you had, you would already know that it is indeed the path to creating the world of your dreams.

Let's take a look at what the medical world calls "the placebo effect." This is the phenomenon in which some people experience health benefits after receiving a placebo, such as sterile water, saline water, a pill, or a fake treatment, all of which could not treat a medical condition. Scientists use these when they are testing new pharmaceutical drugs. When doing research, they will give some patients the drug and others the placebo (or fake drug). None of the patients have any knowledge of what the doctors are doing, and in fact all *believe* they are being given the drug. During this type of research, they have found that just like those patients who had positive results after taking the real drug, other patients who only took the placebo had positive results as well. Why is this? How can that be? One explanation is after taking the placebo, the patient's body released endorphins that act as the brain's own natural pain killers. Another possible explanation includes conditioning and expectation. It is through the thoughts of the patient expecting the drug to work that they receive relief from just using the placebo. This insight into the placebo effect should give you a glimpse of how powerful our minds really are.

Okay, so let's get a little closer to how this *thinking stuff* works. Let's re-visit: How are you to believe you have something when you know you don't have it? Well, this is when we have to go back to our imagination and pretend like we did when we were little kids. Do you remember playing in a tree fort or doll house? Maybe you played with army men, or transformers, or dolls. Whatever it was, you used your imagination to get your mind in a place where you actually believed you were that living, breathing character. In your child-like mind, the fantasy world you created all of a sudden became your reality, and you felt as if you were actually living in that other world. That's where I'm telling you to go. I want you to use your imagination and take yourself to the place you would be, in your mind, if you were in possession of that which you desire. For example, if you want a new mountain bike so you can ride with your friends or co-workers on weekends, use your mind to pretend you already have it. How would you ride it? Where would you go? What color is it? What do the handle bar grips feel like? What does the seat feel like? How comfortable is it? Which friend would you show it to first? How excited would you be? These are all the things you need to think about so you feel as if you already have the mountain bike. When you get to a place in your mind where you actually get goose bumps all over your body because you are truly living the experience through your imagination, then the universe starts moving things around to provide you with that desire.

In Dr. Wayne Dyer's book *Wishes Fulfilled*, which is a fantastic read on how to hone in on your skills of making your wishes come true, he says, "Let go of all doubt, forget about the *when*. It will develop into a material fact on Divine time. Forget about the *how*. Live it inwardly. This is a great power that you possess if you are willing to claim it as your own." What he's telling us here is that we have to feel we already have that which we desire in order for it to come into our physical existence.

This goes for anything you desire. If you want a dress for that upcoming dance, fundraiser, or wedding, you want to know in advance what the dress looks like. What color is it? What style is it? Is it cut above the knees or below the knees? Does it have a V-neck or collar neck? Is it strapless? How does it feel when you have it on? Can you easily dance in it? You want to know all of this and see all of this in your imagination. If you don't know this in advance, you might wind up with any old dress that you may not like, or—worse—end up with no dress at all. Maybe it's a car you want but don't have the money for it. Again, you want to pick out a model and color. What does the inside look like? What does it smell like? How does it drive? What does it sound like? You may think, "Why does all this matter?" Well, it matters because the more you think about the color, style, and sound, the more you will feel yourself in that car, in that dress, or on that bike.

Of course, the more you feel it, the more you start to believe you are actually in possession of it. It's at this level of belief where the magic begins to happen. Don't worry about the "hows," e.g., how can I afford this or afford that? That's not your responsibility. Your responsibility is only to *believe* you have it by using your imagination and feelings. As I mentioned earlier, when you get yourself into a level of belief of already having that which you desire, opportunities will arise and you will be gently prompted to take advantage of these newfound opportunities. Your action in jumping on these opportunities is the gateway towards obtaining your goal. When you get good at this, you'll no longer concern yourself with the "hows" because you'll be attracting the things you want, which to others might appear to be luck, but you'll now know it's not luck at all. It was purely the result of focusing your thoughts in one direction.

Neville Goddard's book *The Power of Awareness* takes the reader deeply into the thinking processes of manifesting one's desires. He talks a lot about what he calls the "Law of Assumption." Neville says, "Willingly identify yourself with that which you most desire, knowing it will find expression through you. Yield to the feeling of the wish fulfilled and be consumed as its victim, then rise as the prophet of *the law of assumption.*" Because the book was written in 1952, some of the youth today might have some difficulty in understanding what he's trying to teach us. In essence, he's telling the reader to pretend and live from a place of already having that which you desire. When you do that, opportunities will arise, seemingly out of nowhere, and you will be prompted to take action in a way that won't feel like work or effort, but rather a feeling of being gently pushed towards doing the things necessary to obtain your goal. This is the opposite of what most of us have been taught, such as work hard, grind it out, and with whatever you have left in your savings, you might be able to purchase what it is you want.

In Joseph Murphy's book *The Power of Your Subconscious Mind*, he includes a story about a blind woman who was living in San Francisco and taking the bus to work each day. One day, the bus route changed, which added almost two hours to her commute. She knew this wouldn't work. But, the only solution she could come up with was driving a car. Of course, she was blind, so driving was not an option. She needed a driver, which she couldn't afford.

So she began fixating her mind on someone driving her to work. Using her imagination and unyielding faith, she created a movie in her head. She heard the car drive up to get her. Her door was opened for her. She felt the seat and heard the noise of the engine. She said thank you to the driver, who she envisioned was a man. The next day her friend read her an article in the newspaper about a man wanting to help the blind. She spoke to this gentleman about her problem. The following day, he stopped and talked to a business owner about this woman's plight. The two of them agreed to drive her to and from work each day. All of this happened within days of her utilizing her mind to come up with a solution. Take notice that she did not stress, work hard towards the goal, or grind it out. What she first did is realize she had a problem. Then she fixated her mind to create a solution. In utilizing the *law of assumption* she drew towards her a solution to her problem. If she had stressed and continually complained about her plight, she most likely would have missed the opportunity for her solution which seemingly came out of nowhere.

STOP HERE

In the previous chapter, you wrote down something you wanted. On the following lines, write down any and all details about what it is you want, where you're getting it, who you're talking to about it, what you're saying, etc. The more details the better.

When I was about 19 years old, I wanted a four-wheel-drive truck, a huge one with a lift kit and large tires. At the time, I was driving this small Volkswagen Rabbit. It was great on gas but not very cool at the time. My friends and I listened to a lot of country music then, and having a truck was high on my priority list. After months and months of searching, I found everything was out of reach due to the prices, but I kept at it. I thought about it daily and virtually every night. My brother had a large truck, and I would borrow his at times just to get the sensation and thrill of driving such a cool rig. I realize many of you readers may not think having a truck is cool, but that's not the point I'm trying to make. I want you to know that when you focus your mind in one direction, you can indeed attract to you anything you desire. One day a friend of mine called me regarding a truck he saw for sale. He drove me over to the location, and thank goodness he did because I would have had no reason to be driving in this neighborhood, and therefore I would have never seen this truck myself. Some of you may not realize this, but at the time there was no internet and no Craigslist or eBay, so people would just put their cars on corners close to their homes with "For Sale" signs on them. I must have called the owner ten times before he called me back. I was nervous because it took forever for him to call me so I figured maybe he sold it to someone else. When he finally called, we met and I bought it on the spot. He told me he had other callers, but his wife had told him he had to call me first because I called more than anyone else. Finally, I had the truck I had been dreaming of constantly.

"Nothing is Impossible. The word itself says I'm Possible."
—AUDREY HEPBURN

Why shouldn't I care about how I'm supposed to get something? If I don't care, then I won't get the money to buy it. This is actually easy to answer, but the reason it seems tricky is because you've never thought about it before. It's like this: If you are concerned with how you are going to get something, then that really means you don't believe you already have it. You see, it all goes back to belief. If you poison your mind with worrying about the "*hows*," then you're making it impossible to truly use your imagination to believe you have it. Memorize this next line, which is one of my favorites: "Fake it 'til you make it." This is one of the most important aspects of this *thinking stuff*. We all must fake it until we make it.

That is, we must believe, through our imagination, that we already have it.

How do we do that? Like I said before, use your imagination and go back to creating the fantasy in your head. See it, feel it, smell it. Find a quiet place to do this. Maybe you should go in your bedroom and close the door. If you share a room, find a time when your sibling is not in there. Sit on your bed, close your eyes, and allow your imagination to take over. See yourself wearing that dress and going to the dance or wedding. Hear all the compliments you're getting from other people in attendance. See yourself riding your new bike. See the trees and smell the air around you. Take your car for a ride. Turn on the radio. Pick up a friend. Do this visualization every day, multiple times a day, and especially just before you fall asleep at night until you know that it's yours. When you believe to the core without any hesitation that you indeed have that which you desire, and it starts to feel natural to you, your subconscious mind will work at making your dream a reality. It must, as Napoleon Hill tells us in *Think and Grow Rich*, because this is a fundamental law of the universe through auto-suggestion, suggesting to yourself over and over that you indeed already have what it is you desire.

In *Wishes Fulfilled,* Dr. Wayne Dyer says, "Because your feelings, especially the feeling of love, are impressed on your subconscious mind, which is responsible for virtually everything that you do, experience, and manifest in your life—your mission is to get to that place of assuming the feeling of the wish fulfilled, even if the wish has yet to materialize in your physical reality."

> "Some things have to be believed to be seen."
> — MADELEINE L'ENGLE

By now you should have a pretty good handle on what faith means, but as I mentioned at the beginning of this chapter, I want to make sure you completely understand the difference between faith and hope. As I do that, it's important to realize how powerful the brain truly is. In laymen's terms, scientists have broken the brain into two parts: the conscious part and the subconscious part. In looking at the difference, you're using your conscious part of the mind to read this book, to think, have conversations, play games, eat, and do other basic activities. The subconscious part of the mind is doing everything else. It controls your body twenty-four hours a day. It keeps the heart pumping, the blood flowing, and the lungs breathing. The best part of all is that it's connected to the all-knowing universe of God. This is of vital importance to understand. It is that connection that brings to you that which you believe you already have.

You see, the subconscious does not know the difference between fantasy and reality. It doesn't discriminate between right and wrong. It responds more like a Genie in a bottle. Remember the story where Aladdin rubs the bottle and out pops the Genie with three wishes? Well, think of your subconscious mind as your personal Genie with unlimited wishes to grant you. Every time you believe and have feelings for a certain thing or situation in life, your personal Genie says, "Your wish is my command." Of course, this is where it can get tricky. Think of your Genie as having stricter controls than Aladdin's

Genie. But that's also why Aladdin's is limited to only three wishes and yours is unlimited. Otherwise, like I mentioned in the first chapter, if you could instantly get anything you wanted, life would ultimately become boring. We are here for the experiences *of* life not for only the material things *in* life. So as you feel and believe that you already have that new dress, that new car, that new boyfriend or girlfriend, the college of your choice, new job or promotion, only then does your personal Genie, the subconscious mind, make the movements within the universe that brings opportunities your way and gives you instinctual messages to take action, so you get in your physical world that which you knew you already had in your imaginary world. These instinctual messages are again like the gentle pushes guiding you toward taking advantage of the newly found opportunities which take you closer to your goal. For example, if better grades are what you are focusing on so you can get into the college of your choice, it could be again that seemingly out of nowhere the smartest person you know calls you to participate in a study group. How did that happen? You don't hang out with this person and you never call this person. Yet, this person called you. That's how this *thinking stuff* works. Because your mind was fixated on a certain goal, opportunities came knocking on your door.

"Belief and faith" then means you're thinking in the present tense: *I am... I have...* "Hope," by itself, on the other hand, is wishing for something in hopes that it comes your way. Any time you say or feel "hope," you have to back it up with belief and faith of already having that which you desire or you are actually jeopardizing your chances of getting what it is you want. Hoping or wishing, by itself, is in the future tense. You're telling yourself you don't currently have that which you desire. Therefore, your Genie is sitting idle. Your Genie is going, "Hmm, wait a minute. Does he want the car? I can't tell. I better sit here and wait a while until he makes up his mind. Oh, there he goes, he's driving it. Okay, I guess he does want it. Oops, he doubts it again. He just said he doesn't have the money. Okay, then he doesn't want it. Oh, he's talking to his friends about it again. He must want it. Oops, nope. He just said his parents don't have the money." You see, when you go back and forth like that (and we're all guilty of it), your genie can't give you what you want. You must believe wholeheartedly. You must initially lie to yourself. Fake it 'til you make it. Keep pretending. Use your imagination. Because when your fantasy becomes a reality, it's no longer a lie. It's a fact.

Again, in *The Power of Awareness*, Neville says, "It is obvious that a lack of faith means disbelief in the existence of that which you desire. Inasmuch as that which you experience is the faithful reproduction of your state of consciousness, lack of faith will mean perpetual failure in any *conscious* use of the law of assumption." What Neville is telling the reader is that without having a deep faith in believing or pretending you already have that which you desire, you then have the exact opposite which is no faith, or disbelief. Therefore, you will continue to reproduce the same results of your past. That is, not obtaining what it is you want.

*"Be faithful in small things because it
is in them that your strength lies."*
➤ *MOTHER TERESA*

You might not want to tell your friends, roommates, or family what it is you are doing. Most people don't like ideas that are different from their own, and most people think their way of doing things is the correct way. I always chuckle at this because if it truly were the case that they have the magic formula to life, well, then their life should look pretty darn good. But since the majority of people aren't too happy with the way things are turning out, they ought to look into other options. Unfortunately, the ego gets into the way, and unless they are seeking some sort of change in their own life, they will only try to pollute yours. There's a saying that carries a lot of truth, and that is "Misery love's company." For this reason, people, even your closest friends and family, will try to pollute your mind by telling you you could never afford this or that. You will never be this or that. In most cases, they don't really know that they are hindering your personal growth, and in fact they sometimes think they are actually help-ing you so you don't get hurt when you don't get what you want. It's only because they haven't read this book or any books like it, which means they don't believe people can attract the things they want in life and therefore you can't either. This is why you shouldn't tell them but rather show them. Wait until you've read enough and practiced enough to start changing your life. When you do that, your friends, co-workers, and family will take notice. When that happens, you can tell them what you're doing and how you're doing it. The truth is, to change this world for the better, we want everyone on the planet to under-stand this *thinking stuff* and learn how to create the world they want. But trust me, it's much easier to show people how it's done, through your own life changes, versus tell-ing them how it's done. Again, this takes practice, and you don't want outside influences to limit your desires. It will happen from time to time, but with practice, you will learn how to minimize it. You were born with the power to create any lifestyle that you desire. I believe in you! The next step is for *you* to believe in you.

Chapter Summary

- When it comes to almost anything, your belief and faith in yourself is a much larger part of making things happen in your individual world than most people think.

- Once you find something this powerful that works and changes your life in so many ways, going back to the old you would be insane.

- If you want something, you have to take action toward that which you desire.

- The harder you work and the smarter you think, the luckier you become!

- I want you to use your imagination and take yourself to the place you would be, in your mind, if you were in possession of that which you desire.

- The more you feel it, the more you start to believe you are actually in possession of it.

- When you get good at this, you'll no longer concern yourself with the "hows," because you'll be attracting the things you want, which to others might appear to be luck, but you'll now know it's not luck at all.

- "Fake it 'til you make it."

- The subconscious does not know the difference between fantasy and reality.

- Belief and faith then means you're thinking in the present tense: *I am . . . I have . . .*

CHAPTER 3

Feeling your goals materialize with emotion

I THINK MOST EVERYONE KNOWS WHAT feelings and emotions are. You know, "I feel tired," or, "I feel happy/sad," or, "I'm so excited I want to jump up and down and scream at the top of my lungs," or, "I'm so happy I could just kiss you." Yes, we all understand what the words mean, but the vast majority of us don't quite understand how powerful our feelings and emotions are.

In the previous chapter, I talked about how we have to use our imagination in order to get what we want in life. Then we talked about how to utilize our belief systems, so we don't become counterproductive in what we want. We all want different things. You want what you want, and I want what I want, and everyone else wants what they want. The funny thing is most of us don't want others to get what they want until we get what we want. I'm sure you've said something, hopefully only to yourself and not out loud, along the lines of, "I don't want McKenzie to get those concert tickets." Of course you don't, because *you* don't have concert tickets. If you did, you probably wouldn't care if McKenzie got hers. Or maybe you didn't want a friend to get a new laptop. Why? Because you don't have one and you want one first. Or maybe you didn't want your friend to get the car she's been talking about. Now you're really angry inside because you know how *out of reach* a car is for you, and how dare she get a car before you? Strangely enough, you haven't really spent much thought on a car because you never thought you would get one. But all of the sudden you deserve one first. In your head you say things like, "She doesn't deserve that car. No way. She's not even that nice to people. She's not even that nice to her parents and in fact complains about her parents all the time. So her parents are going to give a car to a complaining you-know-what, when here I am nice to everyone, never complain, and I get nothing. Something is wrong here."

Well guess what? You're right; something is wrong. You've convinced yourself how great you are and how bad your friend is, and you even said you never complain when in fact that is exactly what you're doing right now—complaining! If you step back and listen to yourself, hopefully you'll realize how bad that sounds. You want a car, all your friends want a car, and in fact most all teens who turn 16 want a car. Even the 17 and 18-year olds with no car want a car, and most everyone who has a license, but no car, wants a car. Now, here you are saying the exact same thing they are, "I want a car," but no one is allowed to have one but you? Oh wait, you say you don't care if the other people you don't know get a car. That's okay because you don't know them anyway. But deep down you don't want your friends to get one before you do; especially the ones who aren't as nice as you. Well, unfortunately you've just made one of the most common, but fatal flaws to your own plan. You want a car and you want to be first, but your friend wants a car and she wants to be first. Your other friend wants a car and he wants to be first. So, who gets to go first? Do you get it yet? If each of you had to be first no one could get their car. Most of your friends think exactly the way you do. Why? Because they have the same habitual thinking patterns you have. You went to the same schools, the same church, lived in the same neighborhoods, watched the same TV shows, and so on. You see, we all have some sort of conditioning, and this conditioning is either helping us achieve what we want, or it's preventing us from achieving what we want. Unfortunately, in most cases, it's not helping. Not because society as a whole is hurting us on purpose, but rather people in society as a whole don't understand how to achieve what they want. All they know is "my way is the right way." Well, as I stated in the earlier chapter, if that were the case, more people would be much happier than they currently are.

So let's go back to the earlier question of who gets the car first. Well, of course it's not quite that simple because there are other factors involved, such as the parents' economic condition, which allows them the ability to buy a car on their kids' 16th birthday, and so they exercise the right to do so. Keep in mind I wrote the previous sentence that way to prove a point. People who have the money have the right to spend it how they wish. Believe me, you don't want anyone telling you how to spend your money, so don't tell others how they should spend theirs. But, if you go back to the previous paragraph, that's exactly what you hypothetically did. You didn't want your friend to get her car first because in your mind you are better than she is, and you should be first. In other words, you're essentially telling her parents not to buy her a car, and therefore you're telling her parents how they should spend their own money. By now you should be realizing how this way of thinking can come back to bite you in the rear.

Let's look at it from another angle. Remember how worked up you got when you found out your friend was going to get a car? Not only were you bummed you didn't have one, you actually became mean and said a lot of hurtful things in your head about this person. You worked yourself up emotionally so that you created very strong feelings of anger and resentment. You even went so far as to convince yourself how you are such a better person than she is, and if your parents could afford to, they would buy you an even better car.

> "Holding onto anger is like
> drinking poison and expecting
> the other person to die."
> ► BUDDHA

Wow, did you hear all that. Here you have a friend who is so excited about getting a car, which is exactly what you wanted so you know how excited she is, and you completely made the story all about you. You've just played an entire movie in your head about how she should not be getting a car and why it should be you.

So, do you really think you'll be getting a car anytime soon? Probably not, but not for the reasons you may have thought. You see, it's not necessarily because your parents can't afford to buy you one (although, that may be the case). In fact, in many cases, parents could afford to buy their teenager a car, but choose not to. It's not necessarily because you may not have earned any money yourself. No, the real reason is because you wouldn't allow anyone else to have what you yourself wanted. Creating deep emotions and feelings about what you think others shouldn't have only prevents you from getting what you want. Like I mentioned earlier, many of your friends think the same way and they also think they deserve to be first, which is also why most of them are not first.

The key word is *allow*. Allow others to want, desire, and achieve what they want. It's their world. As I alluded to earlier on the topic of money, who are you to tell others what they should have and when they should have it? When you allow others to *want what they want*, you are not just doing them a favor, but you are doing yourself an even bigger favor. If you could attract everything you wanted, then you really wouldn't care what other people wanted, would you? Of course not because you would be receiving what you want. So, by allowing others to desire what it is they desire, you have just opened up the flood gates to what *you* want, and things start moving in the direction of achieving those things that you want. Everything moves more freely when there is no restriction of thought, and those thoughts are flowing "in one direction." In essence, you're saying, "You can have what you want, and I can have what I want." This is called "the art of allowing." An important key to remember is one cannot violate the rights of others when he desires something. In other words, if you want my specific and exact car, that's not going to happen unless I freely sell it to you or give it to you, which is probably unlikely to happen. By stealing it, you have violated my rights and your achievement will be short lived. But, it's okay to want one just like mine and purchase one on your own.

STOP HERE

Go back in your memory and write down some situations from your past when you were jealous of someone else getting something you wanted. After you've written these down, let them go. Use the memory only for contrast in now knowing what NOT to do.

This is not a new philosophy. John Locke, born in 1632, is considered one of the most influential political philosophers in the modern era. He defended and claimed that men are by nature free, and argued that people have rights, such as rights to life, liberty, and property. It is within these rights where one should abide by the art of allowing.

Let's go back to the title of this chapter, regarding "feelings and emotions." In the previous paragraphs, we went through in complete detail how your negative emotions can take control of you and actually prevent you from achieving the very same goal your friend might have. Most likely, in this scenario, your friend didn't have negative thoughts of when others were going to get their cars. All she concentrated on was her car. She had pictures in her mind and maybe on the walls in her bedroom. She thought about the car all day every day. She pulled pictures up on the internet constantly. She knew the make, model, and color she wanted. She talked about it all the time at school, at home, and at the dinner table. She imagined herself driving it every day. In fact, she even imagined herself picking *you* up first, right after she got it. She was so excited she wanted *you* to have the first ride. It's been two years of constant day-dreaming about her car. She thinks about it so much she even dreams about it while she's asleep. In fact, both of you are in her dreams driving this very car. Just the thought of the car gives her chills all over her body. She has felt it so much that she knows to the center of her being the car is hers.

"Just be yourself, there is no one better."
▸ TAYLOR SWIFT

Take a look at the two very different stories. Earlier, we talked about the chatter in your head and all of the powerful negative thoughts you might have towards your friend, thinking you deserved the car first. We followed that with all the positive thoughts your friend had on her desire for the car. We all know how the story ends because I've already laid it out. The one who thought about the car tirelessly each and every day with strong feelings and emotions attached to it is the one who achieved her desire in the end.

It doesn't matter what the desire is—be it a car, computer, college, clothing, tickets to something, money, boyfriend, girlfriend, job, or even a spouse. The reason it doesn't matter is, as Napoleon Hill says in his book, *Think and Grow Rich, thoughts become things.* When you think of something with very strong feelings and emotions in a positive manner, things will begin to align themselves in a way for you to achieve your desire. If you ever get the opportunity to talk to a millionaire, an actor, or actress, or a professional athlete, and you ask them how they achieved what they achieved, they will all say the same thing. They first imagined themselves being that person and believed so deeply that they indeed could do and be that which they are doing and being. They felt with such strong emotions and passion that it was already a reality. At this point, as I described in the last chapter, ideas and opportunities starting flowing in their direction. They received those gentle nudges which pushed them to take action toward their desire. But for them this effort was not work as most of us think of *work* in a negative sense. It was as if divine intervention, entangled with the passion of their objectives, created opportunities for them to take any necessary action. They used imagination just like when they were kids to create the make believe world in their minds. After a while, that make believe world becomes reality and they have achieved exactly what they wanted. This is based on Neville's *law of assumption*, which is nothing more than creating thoughts and feelings based on the assumption that you already have what it is you desire or have become who it is you want to become. As you practice this daily, you will eventually master the practice of the law of assumption. You'll know you have mastered it when it feels natural to you that you are already in possession of what you want. At that point, people around you won't believe how lucky you are, but in fact you will know that it wasn't luck at all; you simply maintained focused thoughts in one direction.

Many any of you probably know who the actor Jim Carrey is. He has starred in many blockbuster movies such as *The Mask*, *Dumb and Dumber* and *Ace Ventura*, but it wasn't always like that. Before he hit the big time, there was a point in his life when he was living out of his car. But, he never gave up on his dream. He wrote a check to himself for twenty million dollars, kept it in his wallet, and said that one day he would cash that check. Well, after focusing his thoughts on that dream, that day did indeed come and he was able to cash that check.

STOP HERE

Go back earlier in your childhood and try to recall the times when you wanted that one thing more than anything in the world. Maybe you begged your parents, prayed every night, or both. Write these things down and try to remember how they came about. This will help you in the process of achieving things in the future.

Don't think anything is out of reach for you. You can be or do anything as long as you learn the steps I laid out in this book for you. Take me for instance. How did I write this book, or more importantly, why did I write this book? Why would I spend my time this way when I'm considered by many people to be very successful? I live in a nice home. I've travelled throughout the world. I've jumped out of helicopters onto 12,000-foot mountains just to snowboard where no one else has. I've skied the Austrian Alps. I've scuba dived at Australia's Great Barrier Reef. I've zip-lined in Costa Rica and caught a huge marlin off the coast of Mexico. I even ran with the bulls in Pamplona, Spain. I'm not telling you this to look cool, brag, or have you think favorably upon me. I did all that and more because travel is my passion, and now my passion is to teach as many pre-teens, teens, and young adults how to achieve the life of their dreams.

Don't think you're too young for this. Maybe you're only ten or twelve. This actually makes it easier because you still remember how to pretend and use your imagination. For you teens or adults who are uncomfortable telling others your dreams, don't. Keep it to yourself. This is better because others can't influence you in a negative way and pull you off track from what you truly want and who you truly want to become. Start practicing retraining your thought patterns by working on achieving small things. It makes no difference the size of your desire, but what does matter is your belief system. For instance, maybe you want $50 to buy something, and you don't have $50. Start thinking hard about already having the $50. Pretend you do have it. What is it you're going to buy? Where are you going to buy it? What does it look like, feel like, and even smell like? As you do this, opportunities will come to you. Maybe a neighbor will want you to water his plants while he's on vacation. Maybe your parents will offer you odd jobs around the house, which is something they've never done before. Maybe somebody will give you a one-time chance to deliver magazines and will pay you $50 for the day's work. You see, when you believe you have that which you want, opportunities find you. But, you have to keep your eyes and ears open to listen for them. Now, if you were to say you wanted a $1000 dollars or $10,000 dollars by the end of the week, you would need to be careful. Do you really believe you can do that? Probably not. It's not because it's too much. It's because you *believe* it's too much. Therefore, you most likely will not achieve your desire. This is why you have to use your imagination and "fake it 'til you make it" because your desires will only come to you according to the level of your belief and a natural feeling of already having that which you desire.

For you young adults, it may seem a bit harder to achieve all that you want to achieve, but that is really for one reason and only one reason. It is because you are a bit older than the teens and pre-teens, and therefore, you've had longer exposure to society's conditioning. Thankfully, God has given everyone the ability to create his or her own thoughts. Therefore, even though you have been conditioned by your parents, teachers, friends, and neighbors to put aside your "silly" dreams, you are still given the ability to achieve anything and be anyone you desire by focusing your thoughts in one direction. Just remember to go back to the art of allowing so you don't restrict others' desires and therefore don't restrict yourself. It may take a while to retrain your thinking habits, but you have your whole life ahead of you. So, make it happen according to your own desires. To practice the art of allowing, try pretending you have a mirror in front of you when you're talking about someone else. I had read about this concept a while ago, but I cannot recall who wrote it or which book it came from. The writer's example was for the reader to think of the mirror bouncing the words right back onto you. For example, "I can't believe she got a car. She doesn't deserve it." What did the mirror do? It just bounced those words right onto you and therefore you've just told the universe that you don't deserve a car. Now let's change it up a bit. "That's awesome. Good for her. She's going to have so much fun in that car." Now the mirror, of course, is doing the exact same thing and bouncing those words right back to you. But this time, they are stated in a positive manner, and therefore more good things will be attracted to the speaker of those words. Believe me, this method, which I call the *proverbial mirror method*, works. Use this exercise every time you're talking about someone else and watch your life change rapidly.

Chapter Summary

➤ We all have some sort of conditioning, and this conditioning is either helping us achieve what we want, or it's preventing us from achieving what we want.

➤ Everything moves more freely when there is no restriction of thought.

➤ *Thoughts become things.* When you think of something with very strong feelings and emotions in a positive manor, things will begin to align themselves in a way for you to achieve your desire.

➤ The law of assumption is nothing more than creating thoughts and feelings based on the assumption that you already have what you desire to have or already have become that which desire to be.

➤ Your desires will only come to you according to the level of your belief and a natural feeling of already having that which you desire.

➤ Use the *proverbial mirror method* when you are speaking of others.

CHAPTER 4

Being **present** at all times

HAVE YOU EVER BEEN SOMEWHERE and don't remember much about it? What about driving somewhere but don't remember anything about the drive? Maybe you did something and don't even remember doing it. Every single one of us has had experiences like that. Unfortunately, most of us have these experiences far too often. So why do you think this happens to us? Why don't we remember something right after we did it? The answer is that we are not being present. Sure, our physical bodies are present. They had to be, since we know for a fact we were there. But our minds were somewhere else. So where were they? Where was what you ask? Where was your mind when you were doing this thing you just did? It was wandering. Typically, it's rewinding the past and thinking about things that happened earlier that day, week, month, or even year.

Of course, at other times, your mind just might take you anywhere and everywhere. Maybe you were watching TV and the actors are going shoe shopping. All of a sudden, you started thinking about needing shoes for basketball before the season starts. Then you started thinking about tryouts. "I wonder if I'm going to make the team. Of course I will. I'm a good player. I'm way better than most of the people I know trying out. Will I get the position I want? Sure, I have to. No one else is better than I am in that position. The coach doesn't want to risk losing by putting someone else in my position. That would be crazy. I hope the coach is cool. I remember people talking about how mean he was last year. But I'm sure he'll like me because I'm a cool person. I bet he doesn't like Mark. Mark is always a jerk to people. Why is he even playing basketball? He's horrible at basketball. I remember that one time at the beach when he poured a bucket of water on some lady. It was kind of funny though. What a hot day that was. Man, I haven't been to the beach in a while. I wonder why I haven't gone for such a long time. I should ask my dad to take us this weekend. Why isn't Dad home? It's late. He should be home by now. I wonder what he's doing. What about Joey's dad? He hates the beach. I wonder why he hates the beach so much. Who hates the beach? Maybe he doesn't like the water. I love the water. In fact, I love swimming. Man, I was great on the swim team. I used to win all kinds of ribbons. I wonder what ever happened to Katie. She was a great swimmer. I haven't seen her in, like, forever."

Okay, are you starting to get the point? Here you are watching TV and your mind is wandering. You've gone from shoe shopping to tryouts, to Mark, to the beach, to swimming, to Katie. All this from the trigger of seeing shoes on the TV show you were watching. You did this for about three to four minutes, all while watching your show. Sure, your body was present while it was sitting on the couch with your eyes facing the TV. But your mind was not present. Your mind had wandered off into nowhere land and, like I mentioned earlier, it happens to all of us.

> "Until you take control
> of your life, life will
> take control of you."
> — UNKNOWN

Is it a bad thing when our minds wander off like that? It doesn't have to be, but in some cases it can be detrimental to our success. In a perfect life, we want to be in control of our thoughts. Now, don't get me wrong, because as the first chapter says, it's great to have an imagination. The key is to have our imagination be constructive instead of destructive. Take the example at the beginning of this chapter. For the most part, the mind wandering is fairly harmless. It's not really constructive, but it's not really destructive either. It's your typical run-away mind when you're not too concerned with anything going on in life right now. But, what is a typical wandering mind when there is drama going on in life?

What if this morning at school you just found out your best friend likes the same person you like. You've been angry about it all day. Did you say anything to your friend? No, of course not. You just sat in classes all day stewing over it. In fact, you thought about it non-stop, so you didn't even hear your teachers. Again, your body was present but your mind wasn't. When you went home, you plopped yourself on the couch and turned on the TV, and the show (of course) had two friends, which reminded you of your friend. "I can't believe her. She knows I like him. Why would she do that? She's not my friend anymore. I hate her. A real friend would never do that. I would never do that to her. She doesn't even know him. Not like me. I know him so well. We were meant for each other. He's not going to like her anyway. She's not even that cute. I'm way cuter than she is. That's it. Who needs her? She can go find another friend. I'm telling everyone at school we are no longer friends. I'm not going to summer camp with her this year. She's not even that fun to hang out with. Why did I waste all this time with her?" The mind goes on and on and on. In fact, it will go on for as long as you allow it. I said for as long as *you allow it*. Maybe you're asking, "What does he mean by that?" "Does he really think I can stop it?" Of course you can. Remember, it's *your* mind. But, it takes practice. As I mentioned earlier, we are all conditioned. And that conditioning can be hard to undo. But the funniest part between the two girls liking the same boy is no one ever asked the boy if he liked either of the two girls. I've seen many cases in which the boy doesn't like either girl, which really means all the drama is for nothing. But that's what our minds do to us when we let them run amok. Think about the one angry girl who didn't really listen to her teachers all day during class. Then she doesn't even hear the TV show she was watching with her own two eyes. She went as far as tossing her relationship with her best friend right out the window. All those years of friendship vanished all because of the story she made up in her own head.

STOP HERE

Look back on your day starting from this morning and see if you can recall how many times your mind wandered off. Starting tomorrow morning, keep count of how many times you find your mind wandering off. This exercise will help you learn to focus better on the things you want.

Using slash marks, keep count of how many times your mind wandered each day for the next week.

When I was in high school, I had a girlfriend who was attending a different high school. We lived in the same neighborhood, but I was at our local public school and she was at a private school. She was telling me about this guy who sat next to her in English class and was always bugging her about taking her out. She told him she had a boyfriend, which was me, but he didn't seem to care. Well, after this went on for a while, I was really starting to get angry. Finally, one day I rallied a bunch of my guy friends and we drove over to her school, where we saw him playing tennis for PE class. I called him out for a fight, so we could settle this once and for all to prove that she was my girlfriend and he needed to stay away. He agreed but had to wait until after tennis was over. My girlfriend found us and was crying trying to convince me not to fight. Conversely, my friends were all trying to pump me up to get ready for the upcoming fight. During this time, maybe 30 minutes, my mind starting having different thoughts. Things like, "why am I doing this? She says she doesn't like him, so why should I worry about it? In fact if she did like him, I don't want to be in a relationship with her anyway." After thirty minutes or so, I decided to forget about it and leave. We were either going to stay together or we weren't, but I was going to leave that up to fate. Well, as it turned out, we broke up some months later, which usually happens from time to time in high school. The irony is she ended up marrying the other guy sometime after high school. I'm sure glad I had the presence of mind not to waste the energy or take the chance of getting in trouble for fighting over someone who is no longer in my life.

"I mean, if the relationship can't survive the long term, why on earth would it be worth my time and energy for the short term?"

➤ NICHOLAS SPARKS,
Author of The Notebook

When the mind isn't present, you miss a whole lot of life. You miss a whole lot of opportunities. You miss a whole lot of joy. Not to mention the most important issue, which is that you are not focusing on what you want, therefore keeping what you truly want further away from you. Let me put it another way. Do you think you attract better experiences and things in life on the days you're happy or on the days you're upset and angry? Definitely on the days you're happy. So, when you allow your mind to create a lot of unnecessary drama, you really create a domino effect of negative issues. First, you're not happy. That's a big problem because I believe we are here to enjoy life and be happy. Second, you're not present. You're not enjoying the now, the moment, the only time you have with a guarantee. You see, you're not guaranteed a future, but you do have right now, and you're wasting it on drama. You may have missed the best ballgame of the year. Maybe you didn't notice how beautiful the weather was. Or maybe you didn't see the deer walking in your backyard. Maybe you didn't notice your dog wanting your attention. Whatever might be going on, you completely missed it due to the drama *you* allowed to control your thoughts. Third, you're attracting negativity into your life. Maybe you stubbed your toe or dropped your food on the floor. Maybe your books fell out of your arms and papers flew everywhere. Maybe you missed the bus and now it's going to take a lot longer to get home. Keep in mind these are the little things. The longer one stays angry and/or creates drama, the larger the negative things are that you attract. So, you're not happy and you're not present to enjoy the moment. Instead, you're attracting negative outcomes into your life.

Why would somebody want all that in his or her life? The easy answer is they wouldn't. But, remember, we are creatures of habit, and if we have been conditioned to behave and think in this manner, we'll have a tough time changing unless we make a conscious decision to change. The fact that you're reading this right now is a huge step in the right direction. Because it has taken a while for you to be conditioned in the way you are, it may take a bit of time to reverse that conditioning so you can create the person you want to be and create the life that you want to live. The best part is *you* have all the control. You have the control to read this book or not. You have the control to find other books on the subject. You have the control to befriend the type of people who will help you become a better person. You have the control to put as much effort as needed into making your personal world an incredible place to live. Change your thoughts and change your life.

"We can complain because rose bushes have thorns or rejoice because thorn bushes have roses."
ABRAHAM LINCOLN

Now that you're getting some insight on how you can take back control of your life, do a little, what I call, mind testing. Watch everyone around you. Pay close attention to everyone you communicate with at school, in sports, at work, and definitely within your family or roommates. Also, watch people at the shopping mall and at restaurants. Pay attention to their body language. Did you know that waiters and waitresses at restaurants who smile and have a good time talking with the customers they are serving can make on average almost twice as much in tips as the ones who are bitter, unhappy, and non-engaging? Twice as much just for being friendly. The negative ones typically blame it on getting the bad tables or the bad shifts. Sorry, that's not the reason and it never has been.

At school or work, pay close attention to the peers in your circle of friends or co-workers. Listen to how they talk. Some will love to gossip about others all the time and some just kind of follow along. Some will use sarcasm to put down others just to get laughs from their friends. Others will mock their smart friends for not hanging out with them more often due to studying, and yet they don't mind badgering them for answers on homework and tests. Now isn't that funny? What this simple mind testing does is make you aware of how the majority of people think and therefore act. As you pay attention you'll most likely come to the realization that you, too, think and act in the same manner at times. But that's okay. It's that awareness within you that is going to allow for change.

Let's say the Oscars were on TV the previous weekend, and one of your friends saw a new hairstyle on one of the famous actresses like Jessica Alba. So, she went out the following week to have her hair cut in that same style. When she came to school, she looked fantastic, and everyone was complimenting her. Then you, her so-called BFF, made a joke, saying, "Who does she think she is, Jessica Alba?" and the circle of friends laughed. Your friend heard something said, but she wasn't sure and noticed people were looking at her and laughing. Now she turns and walks away, a bit insecure about her new hair. The question is, why did you say anything negative at all? Especially when you know she looks fantastic. Deep down, you don't really know, but I will tell you in one small word: ego. Ego got in the way and said, "Wait a minute, you're cuter than she is. You're more popular than she is. You need to stop this so people continue to like you better. You don't want the boys to like her more than you, and you don't want your boyfriend looking at her with that new hairstyle." So, you listened to ego and, well, you know the rest of the story. You started this mental anguish on your self-proclaimed best friend who is now insecure with her new hairstyle. It's too bad because she really did look great, but you had to suck the life out of it and take away her thunder.

Let's go back to the earlier chapter where I mentioned looking into the *proverbial mirror*, which just means pretending you're talking into a mirror, anytime you're talking about someone. In the scenario above, what you are really saying is that you're not happy with your own hairstyle. You are not even secure with your friendship, nor are you secure with your boyfriend if you think he is going to easily jump ship because of a new hairstyle on your friend.

It doesn't really matter what the situation is because the reason we all seem to do this boils down to the same answer. It could be two guys competing for the quarter-back position on the football team. Typically what they both do is mock the other one so they can convince everyone else that they are the better candidate. Maybe it's for a student council position at school or a job promotion and the opponents knock each other for the same reason: they want the job. The list is endless, but you know what I'm talking about, and you have your own personal examples you can and should look back at and reflect upon.

STOP HERE

Try to recall times where you have mocked or put down a friend to make yourself look better. Write down who it was about and why. When done, let it go. The purpose is not to focus on the past but rather provide contrast of what NOT to do in the future.

Let's go back to the *why* factor. Why do we do this to each other, especially when we are so-called friends (and in some cases best friends)? Well, the answer is simple, and as I mentioned earlier, it's what I call "habitual thinking habits." From the time we are born, those surrounding us—such as family, friends, neighbors and teachers—have been slowly conditioning us to think the way they do. It always amazes me that we are conditioned to constantly talk badly about the very people we call our friends. What's even more amazing is I used to be one of those people. Maybe not to the same degree as some, but nonetheless, I am definitely guilty of doing the same thing. The best part is that we can change. I know this to be a fact because I did. It takes practice, of course, because just like your old habits took a while to become habits, it will take some time to create new habits. But every single one of you can start taking back control of your lives as long as your desire is to learn how to attract everything you want and deserve out of life. After all, you're here, so you might as well figure out how to make your world incredible.

"Life isn't how to survive
the storm, it's about how
to dance in the rain."
➤ TAYLOR SWIFT

So how does this tie into the chapter title of living in the now and being present? The answer lies in your thoughts. You've been consumed by gossiping about others and knocking others down so as to look better in front of your peers, and you've lost sight of what you truly want. What you truly want is to be happy, be confident, be student council President, be quarterback, secure the starting position, be comfortable with your boyfriend or girlfriend, get promoted, and the list goes on. But, when you're spending time, energy, emotions, thoughts, and feelings on knocking someone else down, you're burning up valuable time in your day where you could and should be focusing on your own world. Just as in the previous chapter where we talked about having to have a car first, you need to let go. Once you let go and allow others to have what they want, you can begin to spend your time and energy focusing on what you truly want, and magical things will begin to happen.

Let's look at an example of two people competing for a position on the volleyball team. (For those of you looking for a new job or promotion, you can easily substitute the verbiage in this example to apply in the workplace.) One is solely focused on letting the best person win and focusing intensely on making himself or herself a better player. The other is focused on mocking the other player in front of the teammates and working herself or himself to get closer to the coach. Now that you've read most of the book, who do you think is going to get the starting position? That's right. The one who used the *proverbial mirror method*, I mentioned earlier, and didn't try to knock down the other person is most likely to get the starting position because they are generating the most positive energy. Having said that, there are always exceptions. Maybe the other player did get close to the coach and won the coach over. Maybe the coach overlooked the fact that the other player was better but gave the position to the brown-noser. When this happens, and unfortunately it does from time to time, stay the course. Don't change who you are by talking negatively about the other player. Keep working hard, practicing hard, and playing hard. Most always, a shift takes place. Either the brown-noser gets hurt, has a family emergency, goes on vacation, or whatever, and you all of a sudden get your chance to start. At this point, you are noticeably the better player, and all the parents are talking about how good you are. Finally, the coach will typically move you permanently into that starting position. I can't stress enough importance of not falling into the trap of behaving like the brown-noser player. As the saying goes, "What goes around comes around." Eventually, karma bites them in the rear and they don't understand what hit them. But you'll know exactly what happened. They didn't use the *proverbial mirror method*, and the negative vibes they were broadcasting finally came back to haunt them.

"I saw that."
➤ KARMA

So how would one define being present? I would say that being present is knowing who you are, what you are, and where you are at all times. When you are consciously aware of those three things at any given moment, then you are considered present in that moment. When we gossip about others, we are not present. We are lost and allowing ego to take over. When we speak negatively about others, we are not present and ego again has taken over. When we are gripped with fear and insecurity, we are not present and once again ego has taken over.

Let's take another look at why we are the way we are. Do a mind test on your family or roommates. For the next two weeks, pay close attention to how your parents speak to you, your siblings, friends on the telephone, relatives, neighbors, and the overall general public. Pay attention to how your siblings speak to each other and how they talk about their friends. Of course, pay attention to your own personal thoughts and what comes out of your own mouth. As you do this, you'll be amazed to learn why things happen to people. If your family is very negative, and you're one of those people, you will start to learn why everything isn't so blissful in the household. You might notice your father yelling at the TV because he doesn't like the information on the news. Then he starts mocking the people in the story as ego has taken a grip on his thoughts and he is not present. Within minutes, you might see something you would have never paid attention to before. Maybe he spills his drink. Maybe he bumps into the coffee table. Maybe nothing happens right away, but then he drops something at the dinner table. Just watch and pay attention. No one is immune to attracting negative things in their lives, and when ego is in control, look out because here it comes. Maybe it's a speeding ticket or a car accident. Oh I know, it wasn't his fault. The officer was a jerk or the other guy caused the accident. Sorry, it doesn't work that way.

When we are habitually negative in life, we attract negative things into our lives. Of course, they don't match one for one, meaning if I wished you to roll an ankle on the soccer field so I could play, it doesn't mean I'm going to roll my ankle. What typically happens is something completely different and random happens to you, which is why most people are oblivious to the fact that the negative thoughts one has toward others and the random negative events which occur in that person's life are related. Well, I have news for you. They are most certainly related, and until one understands and learns how to take back control of his or her conscious thoughts and stay present, he or she is destined to go through life with these so-called "random events" plaguing him or her.

STOP HERE

Pay attention to how members of your family talk and act. Write down the positive and negative events that take place over the next week. This will help you pay attention to your own thoughts as you notice the patterns of those around you.

At the end of the book, I have provided some short cuts on how to stay present and learn to control your conscious thoughts by focusing them in one direction. But as I said earlier, it takes practice. If you choose not to study this material and not practice creating new thinking habits, you are choosing to keep your world the way it is. It's always your choice.

Chapter Summary

➤ The key is to have our imagination be constructive instead of destructive.

➤ When the mind isn't present you miss a whole lot of life. You miss a whole lot of opportunities. You miss a whole lot of joy.

➤ When you allow your mind to create a lot of unnecessary drama, you really create a domino effect of negative issues.

➤ We are creatures of habit, and if we have been conditioned to behave and think in this manor, we'll have a tough time changing unless we make a conscious decision to change.

➤ Change your thoughts and change your life.

➠ Every single one of you can start taking back control of your lives as long as your desire is to learn how to attract everything you want and deserve out of life.

➠ Once you let go and allow others to have what they want, you can begin to spend your time and energy focusing on what you truly want, and magical things will begin to happen.

➠ Being present is knowing who you are, what you are, and where you are at all times.

CHAPTER 5

Making your **dreams** come true

DREAMS ARE MORE IMPORTANT THAN you realize. Have you ever thought about what a dream really is? I don't mean the kind of dream you have in your sleep— although some can be great. I mean the kind of dream dreamers have. Those larger-than-life fantasies that sometimes seem so out of reach, a lesser minded person might consider it a waste of time. Someone who calls dreaming a waste of time couldn't be farther from the truth. The fact is, everything starts with a dream. Enzo Ferrari created one of the most renowned car companies in the world; his dream was to create the fastest racecar in the world, and he did just that. It wasn't logical or even practical from a business perspective, but then again, most dreams aren't logical at all. I mean, who wants to put everything on the line and take a chance of losing it all and going broke? Dreamers, that's who!

Let's go back to some of the earlier chapters where first we talked about the scenario with the car. You wanted the car, but your friend got the car first. Why? Because it was her dream. She thought about it endlessly. She had pictures on her bedroom wall and would draw the car while doodling during history class. When she was a passenger in a car with her friends or family, she would picture herself behind the wheel of her car. When her mom was driving her to the store, in her mind, it was really she driving her mom in her new car. When her dad was taking her to school, it was really she driving her dad in her new car. That's what dreamers do. They take any and all possible time to focus intently on what it is they want by thinking in one direction. This takes little energy and doesn't cost anything. All it takes is a vivid imagination and the determination to keep dreaming non-stop.

So, why is dreaming really important? Well our planet would be very boring if we didn't have dreamers. We wouldn't have cities if dreamers didn't dream about them first. We wouldn't have ski resorts if someone didn't dream about them and make it happen. There wouldn't be shopping malls as you see them today if we didn't have dreamers. We wouldn't have Major League Baseball, the NBA, the NHL, or the NFL if we didn't have dreamers. What about some of the places you've been to while on vacation as a child? Does Disneyland come to mind? For Walt Disney to create such a magical place for children, and to think up the characters and all the movies kids have enjoyed for decades, it definitely took a lot of dreaming.

Are you starting to understand why dreams are so important (probably more important than you realized)? I hope so, because we need you to be the next big dreamer. In fact, we all rely on each other to dream so our world creates more incredible people, places, and things for all of us to enjoy.

"The future belongs to those who believe in the beauty of their dreams."
— ELEANOR ROOSEVELT

In the previous chapter, we talked about how gossiping or being negative towards others attracts negative things to enter into our own lives, and we covered how we can minimize it by using the *proverbial mirror method*. But, how do we stop others from squashing our dreams? Why do we allow them to do it? I used the word allow because it's the truth. No one, not your mother, father, teacher, best friend, sibling, grandfather or grandmother can keep you from dreaming. But in many cases they will infiltrate your mind with what many would call *mind pollution*. *Mind pollution* really means what it sounds like. Think about pollution in the air from factories and cars. It wreaks havoc on the environment. *Mind pollution* works in the same way. The more negative thoughts that enter your mind, the more pollution you have in your mind, which is preventing you from your dream. Let's look at some examples.

Say you love baseball. You've played for years in little league, and you currently play at the high school level. In your mind all you want to do in life is play baseball. In fact, you want to play for the New York Yankees. When you watch games on TV, you see yourself playing your position.

When you're up to bat, you picture yourself hitting a home run. You close your eyes and picture yourself rounding the bases and jumping on home plate as the rest of the dugout comes out to high five you on your game-winning home run. You know the stats on all the players, and you even know the umpires by name. As a child you would tell your parents that you were going to play for the NY Yankees some day and they would just smile. Now you're a teenager and you're still telling them you want to play for the Yankees. But, now you notice facial expressions that are different. It's the kind of look that makes you think they don't believe in you. Maybe it's not that they don't believe you want to, but deep down they don't believe you can. They think it's a fantasy too far out of reach, and they don't want you to get hurt by being disappointed.

> "Never give up on a dream
> just because of the time it
> will take to accomplish it.
> The time will pass anyway."
> •ANONYMOUS

So, what just happened to you? Well, for most, what happened was your dreams were crushed. It's not that your parents slammed you down and told you to forget about it, although plenty of parents and others do that to us dreamers. Rather, you read their body language and you knew they didn't believe in you. Unfortunately, you allowed them to squash your dream. I want to stress that in many cases it doesn't take a whole lot to push us away from our dreams. As humans, it's in our nature to want others to like and believe in us. If we feel our parents don't believe in us, then most of us give up and start moving in a direction our parents think might be best for us. Unfortunately, this can be disastrous.

Another point I want to stress is that your parents just want what is best for you. Having said that, I recognize they might not truly know what is best for you. It could be they grew up poor and they never want to see you struggle. But, you're an artist, and they are both attorney's. They want you to become a lawyer also so you'll have financial freedom. It's not that it's a bad idea; they know the financial freedom they have enjoyed by becoming attorneys. Because of that drive for financial success, they push you into taking more difficult classes at school. They push you on grades. They push you to read all the time during weekends, school breaks, and during the summer months. You, of course, are becoming a good reader and have increased your vocabulary dramatically. There's only one problem. You're an artist! You see, you didn't grow up poor. You grew up enjoying life and taking art classes as a child, which really helped you become a great dreamer. Now you feel like your parents are killing your dream so you can be like them. That would make them proud. But you're not as happy as you used to be. Maybe you start sabotaging your school work, and your grades drop. Maybe you blow off studying for finals. After you do this for a year or two, your parents begin to give up hope on your going to law school. In fact, they wonder if you can get into any college at this point, and now the goal is just for you to finish high school. The last couple years have been horrible, and all you do is fight and argue with your parents. You either want to hide out in your room or not go home at all. Unfortunately, by sabotaging school to defeat your parents, you ended up ruining your own chances on getting into a good art school. You got involved with the wrong kids just to prove a point with your parents, but in the end you only hurt yourself. The bummer is, you can't go back in time to change anything. What you can do is make a decision to turn yourself around and start re-focusing on your dream.

So what happened? Well, a couple things. First, your parents made the mistake, which I have seen many parents do, thinking you should be just like they are. You, on the other hand, made the mistake of not sitting down with your parents and explaining how art is your passion; it's in your blood. Being an attorney does not excite you. It is art that excites you. Of course, I realize that most teens aren't going to know how to convey this message to their parents, but hopefully after reading this book, you'll be able to do just that. I believe that once you learn what I'm telling you here, you'll be able to articulate and explain exactly what it is you want to do, why you want to do it, and also why it could be problematic for you and your parents to push their dreams on you. Again, please do not blame your parents or think they are wrong. They are just doing what we parents do, which is to try to push our kids to be the best they can be. For most parents out there, they may not have read any books on this subject and therefore just believe that what they are doing is the right thing. That's okay because it comes from a place of love. But, it's your job to let them know what *your* dream is and why it's important for all of us to follow our dreams. What will help your case is having a deep understanding of what I've laid out in this book. As you learn this knowledge well enough to change your habitual thinking, it will be much easier to sit down with your parents and tell them your dreams. In fact, many of you will even get your parents support, whereas you might not have earned it before you gained this knowledge.

> "Do not follow where the path
> may lead. Go instead where there
> is no path and leave a trail."
> — RALPH WALDO EMERSON

STOP HERE

Write down your dreams. Maybe you know what you want to do as an adult. It could be the college you dream of attending. Just remember, it's your dream, so make it a good one.

....

....

....

....

....

....

The first thing to realize is that it takes passion to be truly successful. Very few people become successful when doing something they don't like. Of course, there will be cases in which people have become financially successful when doing something they would rather not be doing, but that is a rare exception. Passion drives creativity, and it's creativity that allows innovation to bloom. Of course, it's innovation that consumers want to see because we like to buy new things all the time. If our cell phones never changed, we would only buy new ones after our current ones broke, instead of every time a new model comes out. If cars didn't change, we would only buy new ones after we drove them into the ground. Take a look at clothing. It's always changing because consumers are always looking for something different. Things get boring and tired. Buying new products is fun and exciting for all of us. What the parents in the hypothetical scenario didn't realize is that it takes artists to create those new products. It wasn't an attorney who created the look of the iPhone. Nor was it a real estate broker who created the Nike swoosh logo, one of the most recognized logos in the world. I'm pretty confident that an insurance broker didn't design the latest motorcycle to come out of West Coast Choppers. You see, it's not that being an attorney or a real estate broker aren't great occupations for some, because they are. But, if you're an artist, you need to follow your dream if you want to realize what true success feels like.

How many of you have seen the TV show *Shark Tank*? What a fantastic show to teach young and old alike how the minds of investors, "the Sharks," work. Even I, one who has invested in many companies, have learned a lot from the show. If you pay attention, what you'll observe is how passionate the people are when they bring their product into the Shark Tank. Many of them work day and night to turn their product into a reality. Does it always work, and do they always walk away with a deal from one of the Sharks? Of course not. But, as the Sharks normally tell them, keep working on it and something will happen. Maybe it's too early for them to step in. Maybe they themselves don't believe in the product, and that's okay. Have you ever heard of Colbie Caillat? She was rejected twice by American Idol and was unable to sing for the judges. She has since sold over six million albums worldwide and ten million singles. Thank goodness she didn't give up after being rejected. There are plenty of stories like this, when others did not believe in one's product, but fortunately the inventor or artist did not give up because millions of other people did love the product. It goes to show you that even wealthy business people, including the Sharks, don't have a magic ball that always gives them the right answer. They take risks and gamble as long as they believe in the product and the inventor has passion. I saw one show where a family was in the lumber business somewhere on the East Coast. The sons of the father had an idea of taking their discarded lumber and creating sunglasses out of them. No two pair are alike due to the grain of wood. When I saw the show, I loved the idea. Others, of course, with a logical mind, might say the sunglasses market is oversaturated and too competitive, which will make it too hard to break into that market. If an inventor hears that from someone and doesn't have real passion for his product, he's likely to give up before he even starts. That's a shame because, like I mentioned before, dreams are not always logical. Just last week my daughter told me she saw the glasses at a store called Tilley's. I laughed inside and thought, "What a wonderful dream."

> *"If you can imagine it, you can achieve it. If you can dream it, you can become it."*
> — WILLIAM ARTHUR WARD

The second most important factor to realize is that while one is following his or her passion, and the creative juices are flowing within him or her, things just seem to fall into place. As I mentioned in the chapters on faith and feelings, people come out of nowhere to help you get to the next level. There is very little friction when you are moving in the direction that feels natural to you. You will be in a happier state of mind a majority of the time, and as I pointed out in an earlier chapter, being happy attracts positive situations in your life, just like being miserable attracts negative things in your life. What I'm trying to explain here is that this is how the universe is designed. Events are not random. If you focus your thoughts intensely in one direction on what it is you want to achieve and take the action necessary when internally prompted to do so, without compromising your integrity or taking advantage of another person, events in your life will be altered so as things move in your direction.

Maybe you helped a lady with her groceries after she dropped a bag in the parking lot, and the two of you started talking. Come to find out she is the principal of the high school you are dying to get into. Or maybe you're at a restaurant with three of your friends and they seat you at a larger table for six. A family behind you needs a table for six, so you convince your friends to give your table to them. A conversation starts up, and it turns out the gentleman is an executive at Apple Computer Company, which is where you have been trying to get an interview and dream of working. You see, you're not going to be sent an email or a text saying, "At six p.m. this evening you are going to bump into this man who is an executive at Apple, so please talk to him to get your future job." Sorry, it doesn't work that way. In fact, if life were that easy, it would be boring and take the fun out of living. All you have to do is focus on what you want, stay present, and always do the right thing for others. When you do this, your life will magically change, and your friends will think you're the luckiest person they've ever met.

This is the very reason why people should follow their dreams. When we go against our own instincts and our own personal desires, the vast majority of us are doomed to mediocrity at best. You're young, which is why you may not realize that the majority of adults working would rather be doing something else—most are not happy in their current job but feel trapped. Most all of them had dreams when they were younger, but they lost sight of those dreams. They started working in jobs that really didn't challenge them or make them happy. It was just a job to pay the bills. Similarly, what happens when one tries to swim upstream or against the current in a river? He won't get very far and will tire out quickly. Eventually, the stream will push him past where he started. That's a great metaphor in saying that when you do things against your instinctual feelings, you won't get too far, and you might even go backwards. Some might say you could drown in a sea of negative situations. Stay the course and follow your instincts. It's your instincts that God gave you to achieve your dreams.

> "Your talent is God's gift to
> you. What you do with it
> is your gift back to God."
> ▸ UNKNOWN

You are young, which is why it is my passion to get you this information before your habits are hardened and possibly enter the wrong career path for the remaining balance of your life. Did you know that only 5% of the people on this planet control almost 90% of the world's wealth? My point in telling you this is certainly not to turn you off by thinking you don't have a chance, because nothing is further from the truth. You have a better chance than most just by learning the techniques I've outlined in this book. What that math shows is that very few people have figured out how to channel their thoughts in one direction and achieve their goals. Follow your dream! Not only can you change your own personal world, but you can help enhance the world for others.

Chapter Summary

- Take any and all possible time to focus intently on what it is you want by thinking in one direction.

- We all rely on each other to dream, as we need more incredible people, places, and things for all of us to enjoy.

- The more negative thoughts that enter your mind, the more pollution you have in your mind, which is preventing you from your dream.

- What you can do is make a decision to turn yourself around and start re-focusing on your dream.

- It's your job to let your parents know what *your* dream is and why it's important for all of us to follow our dreams.

- It takes passion to be truly successful.

⟫ Passion drives creativity, and it's creativity that allows innovation to bloom.

⟫ You need to follow your dream if you want to realize what true success feels like.

⟫ There is very little friction when you are moving in the direction that feels natural to you.

CHAPTER 6

Learning to **feel natural** while making your goal a reality

AS I MENTIONED BEFORE, I have read a number of books in the area of self-help, which have completely transformed the way I think. It's not as though people didn't consider me to be *normal* prior to my learning this *thinking stuff*, but that truly was the problem. I was normal! I thought and behaved like most people did. Fortunately for me, I wasn't satisfied with being this so-called *normal*. I wanted a larger understanding of how the mind, body, world, and universe worked. I went to church my whole life, and still I was confused about why things are the way they are. I always wondered why God doesn't just change things to make life easier for everyone. I wanted to know why so few people were financially successful and why so many more were not. Why were so many people getting cancer than in years past? What about the divorce rate? Why was it so high compared to decades ago? Everything seemed to be changing, for the worse, and I wanted to make sure those things didn't happen to me.

The truth is, as I read and studied the areas of the subconscious mind as well as religion, the answers did come. Although, I think it's actually hard to explain to someone who hasn't read any of the books on the subject because when you really understand what I've been teaching in this book, you'll realize it's not so much that you *know it* as it is you *feel it.*

Throughout the book I have talked about the importance of using your imagination and then having belief and faith in what it is you imagine doing or having. This faith must then be backed up by strong feelings of desire for what it was you want. I then spoke about being present and how to stay present so you don't get pulled into gossip or allow ego to control your thoughts. As I personally learned this, I only then understood how important dreams were. In fact, I had been to plenty of motivational seminars where the speakers would tell the audience to "dream big" and "not limit your dreams at all. Go for it like you never thought you could."

When I was 23 and just out of college, my mother took me to a seminar where Roger Palmieri, author of *Dream Big I Dare You: Better Yet I Double Dare You*, was speaking. This was the first seminar I had ever attended. I was mesmerized. I had no knowledge of this *thinking stuff* at the time, but there I was glued to every word about dreams. To this day I still remember him saying, "If you want to live in a certain neighborhood, you should be driving home through that neighborhood as if you live there." As you recall from the first chapter, I did have a specific neighborhood I wanted to live in, and from then on, I modified my route home and eventually bought my house in the neighborhood I wanted.

I had dreams bigger than I ever thought possible with the old me. The old me would have said I was crazy to dream that big. But the new me said, "Why not?" So, I created big dreams and focused on them over and over again. The only problem was they weren't coming as quickly as I would have liked. This was a bit troubling, but I didn't want to sabotage my dreams by second guessing myself. Nevertheless, I felt like something was missing. As it turned out, something was missing, and it was a key ingredient in the way one needs to think in order to bring his desire to him. That simple ingredient was that *natural feeling* we all get when something feels right.

As I stated earlier, we must have dreams and use our imagination vividly to bring those dreams to life. But when our dreams are really big—like wanting to be a professional athlete or the world's top model, providing fresh water to the poor villages throughout the world, or becoming the next rock star or rapper, next great computer software programmer, or next Mother Teresa who helps make the world a better place—it must feel natural to you in order to bring them to life. By "feel natural," I mean you must believe that you are already that which you desire to be. Think about this way: If you play football now, it feels natural to be on the team. It feels natural to go to practice. It feels natural to hang out with other players from the team. All of this feels natural because it's happening in your physical world now. It makes sense to you that it feels natural, just as living in your house and sleeping on your bed feels natural. It's because you do it every day. Maybe you're in band at school and also play in a private band after school with friends. Both feel natural to you because you are currently in both bands in your current physical reality.

What if you could harness that natural feeling and use it for something that is not in your current physical world just yet? Obviously, if you're in middle school or high school, you would be too young to play in the NFL, NHL, or NBA. But that's okay because you need time to practice, work out, grow, and truly understand this *thinking stuff*. This gives you more time to use your imagination so you can get yourself in a state of feeling natural about being on that team. What if you wanted to get fresh drinking water to everyone on the planet, water that most of us in the United States take for granted? At age 15, you might see that as an enormous undertaking,

but I don't want you to think about the potential diffi-
culties. To worry is to sabotage progress and possibly
stifle your dream. Just start by seeing villagers in these
poor countries not having to walk miles only to be able
to return with the amount they can carry. Picture them
having fresh water wells within their villages. Think
about how that might help them prosper, minimize dis-
ease, and contribute to producing more field crops to feed
their people. Now multiply that by many more villages
in additional countries and watch how *your* dream has a
huge positive impact on the world. Those are the kinds of
thoughts that propel dreams into reality.

You may feel young now, but take advantage of this
time to study and learn about government and politics.
Maybe you should make a list of the countries you want
to start with and prioritize the list in some manner. Over
time, you will see amazing things unfold, like being in-
troduced to the right people who share your cause, or
maybe befriending someone who invented something
but doesn't know what to use it for and, voila, you have
what you need to provide fresh water to these people. It's

by maintaining your thoughts in this one direction that the answers come to you. What if being a millionaire is what you wanted? Do you think it's out of reach? Do you think you can't do it? Is that too much? The fact remains that when you concentrate your thoughts and get yourself feeling natural about your desire with the steps I've laid out in this book, *anything* is possible.

As I mentioned in the previous paragraph, it may be that you are too young to achieve those large life goals right now. But that shouldn't keep you from working toward your dreams because, before you know it, you will be old enough to effect change. Use this time to practice and hone your skills on achieving smaller dreams. Work on the little things like a clothing item you want, tickets to a concert you covet, a starting position on the team, your dream date, or a family vacation. As with anything, the more you practice achieving your smaller goals, the more confidence you will gain towards achieving your larger goals. Many of you might already be working in your first or even second job after college, but want to be doing something different. That's okay, but be the best you can be in your current job and opportunities will arise. While you take this time learning more work skills, seek out new books or seminars and study this *thinking stuff*.

But I must warn you. Don't chase after money for the sake of money. This typically prevents people from achieving their goals. I have seen, read about, and had personal friends who have chased after money, and some who have acquired it, but at the cost of getting divorced, spending little time with their kids, getting cancer, having heart attacks, and even dying too young from all the stress of chasing money. Instead, find something you're passionate about. It's the passion within you that will drive your success, and through that passion you will have the right attitude to make things happen and make the money appear. The key here is not to worry about the money. To worry means you're true belief is coming from a place of lacking true passion and therefore, as I've mentioned earlier in the book, the money eludes you. The main difference here is when you do something with passion driving it, it doesn't feel like work. In fact, it feels like fun. Take me for example. I've spent well over a year writing this book. Because I have my current profession, I have to write in the early morning, at night, on weekends, and sometimes even on vacations. But guess what? It doesn't feel like work. In fact, quite the opposite. I'm enjoying the whole process. It's exciting for me to get this information into the hands of as many young people as possible because that's how *I'm* trying to make the world a better place. It's learning through examples like this, and the many others out there that are driven by passion, that will help you avoid all the built-up stress I mentioned earlier. In fact, when you use this knowledge, you'll create a life most others will envy. So, while you have this time in school, take this time to read, study, and practice using your imagination to get you to a place of feeling natural.

"When you get to a point where you think you have all the answers, that's when you've lost your imagination."

➤ TODD J COURTNEY

I want to reiterate what I mentioned regarding money as a dream. Typically you want this because your family does not have a lot of money and you've seen first-hand how stressful that can be on a family. Believe me; I understand this. It is through your physical reality of living in that household that you have indeed been conditioned to believe that money is hard to come by. It has been *normal* in your world to have financial issues. The problem with this normalcy is the majority of us grow up creating that same normalness, the same *normal* reality of having financial issues that we really don't like.

So how do we break the cycle? How does one grow up and get out of the financial stress they have been accustomed to? Is it education? For many the answer is yes, but not for everyone. Is it a trade? Again, for many the answer is yes, but it's not for everyone. The answer lies beyond education, hard work, and diligence. The answer is laid out in this book, especially in this chapter: most of all, your desire must feel natural. If whatever it is you want doesn't feel natural, then it will forever elude you. "Is this easy?" you ask. For many it's not, but it's what God means when he says everyone is equal. Every time you've heard your parents, grandparents, teachers, or whoever say you can do anything and become anything, this is where the meaning comes from. Yes, you can, but whatever it is you want, that desire must feel natural to you.

Growing up in a household with six kids, I don't have to tell you money was tight. Mom took us kids shopping at the beginning of the school year to get clothes and shoes. They had to last, of course, because we weren't getting new ones until the following year. When it came to food, our house was rarely stocked. Does anyone out there like rice? Well my dad would buy 50-pound bags of it, and we ate it all the time. What about macaroni and cheese? Oh yeah, that was a main staple in our household. How about milk that didn't need a refrigerator? Say what? That's right. It was powder out of a box we would mix with water to create milk. You ever have spam? Sorry Hawaiian's, I know it's a delicacy in Hawaii, but for us it was mystery meat. My point in telling you all this is that this was my normal. In fact, for all six of us kids, it became our normal. We were conditioned to believe that this was the way it was. Of course, when you get outside your house and visit a friend who has milk from a real cow, you start to realize that life doesn't have to be like the "normal" you have come to accept and expect.

So what did I do to change my normal? I made it my mission not to accept that way of life. I had dreams in my head all the time about what I wanted and how I wanted to live. In fact, it got to a point where I truly knew in my heart that I was going to have more than I grew up with. I was so confident that I was going to be financially successful that when I prayed, I wished that all my family and friends would be more financially successful than I. The reason I prayed like that was because I knew to the core of my being that I was going to be successful and I didn't want anyone to get left behind. So I came up with that prayer. Ironically, I didn't know anything at the time regarding the information in this book and the many like it. But if you recall some of the stories in the previous chapters, in which the person wanted to be first and would be negative toward anyone who was a threat to him, I was the exact opposite. I was just like the girl who got the car. I focused on my dream and got to a point of feeling natural about achieving my dream. In fact, it felt so natural that I prayed for everyone around me to achieve more than I did. Of course, I didn't know that people were in charge of their own destiny, so I thought my prayers would help. The truth is, it helped me. It helped me because I had no resistance with anyone else trying to achieve success. It helped me because the universe answered in the form of reciprocation. I gave positive thoughts for others to prosper, and in return I prospered.

So please, don't think you're too young or too old to start believing in yourself. Don't think you're too young to be a professional athlete, rock star, top model, savior who provides drinking water to third world countries, auto mechanic with multiple locations, or artist creating incredible pieces of art that the world craves. Don't limit yourself. Follow your dreams and use your imagination vividly so you too can feel natural in your new *normal*. All of this and more can happen by "focusing your thoughts in one direction."

Conclusion

In conclusion, I want you to know that there always has been, and probably always will be, critics in the world who will try to convince others that this *thinking stuff* doesn't work or is just made up fantasy. The irony is most of these critics don't have the perfect balance of health, wealth, and happiness. So, if you ever feel you're falling victim to any of these critics and start believing they or you have all the answers, do what I do and Dr. Phil yourself. That is, just say, "How's that working for you?" It's that simple self-examination that will give you the answer you're looking for.

Chapter Summary

➤ When you really understand what I've been teaching in this book, you'll realize it's not so much that you *know it* as it is you *feel it*.

➤ Don't sabotage your dreams by second guessing yourself.

➤ Whatever it is you are dreaming, it must feel natural to you in order for you to bring that dream to life.

➤ To worry is to sabotage progress and possibly stifle your dream.

➤ It's by maintaining your thoughts in this one direction that the answers will come to you.

➤ It's the passion within you that will drive your success, and through that passion, you can work to make the money appear.

➤ The more you practice achieving your smaller goals, the more confidence you will gain towards achieving your larger goals.

➤ If whatever it is you want doesn't feel natural, it will forever elude you.

➤ Give positive thoughts for others to prosper, and in return you will prosper.

Mind Shift Tips

BELOW ARE SOME TECHNIQUES AND examples on how to create a mind shift and create an affirmation for things you want to achieve. Please visit our website at www.teenscandream.com for more examples and a collection of short stories to help you achieve whatever it is you want. Our short stories cover a variety of topics such as being a better test taker, attracting a date for the prom, or improving your game in most sports, as well as sections on handling bullying, peer pressure on alcohol, drugs, and sex, and the stress of applying to colleges. Our mission is to help as many teens as possible by teaching them to think their way to a better life.

Mind shift on negative thoughts

PROVERBIAL MIRROR METHOD: At the end of chapter three, I talked about imagining having a mirror in front of you when you're talking or thinking about someone else. Any negative thoughts or words are bouncing off the mirror and back onto the person thinking or saying those thoughts. Use this concept to minimize your negative thoughts or negative conversations about others.

Mind Testing

MIND TESTING: In chapter four on being present, I explained how mind testing works. Pay attention to how your friends at school talk and watch their body language. Do the same thing at home with your family. Take notice of what they say and how they say things. You'll begin to observe how everything I've written in this book does indeed happen in the way I've laid things out. Unfortunately, what you'll notice is that most people speak on the negative side and don't understand the proverbial mirror method. Observe how they attract situations to them that they would rather not be a part of. Yet, they blame outside influences for all the negative that comes their way.

Mind Shift on Staying Present

STAYING PRESENT WITH THANK YOU MODE: When your mind wanders, which—if you're like me—it will try to all the time, I suggest you create a *mind shift* to pull yourself to the present. I call it the *thank you* mode. I use it like this. Let's say I'm driving down the road and negative thoughts start popping in my head. When I realize what is happening, I immediately go into the *thank you* mode. That is, in my head, I say "thank you" for anything and everything that is around me. This is very simple and yet very effective.

EXAMPLES: If I'm in my car, I say thank you for the radio; thank you for the steering wheel; thank you for the engine; thank you for all the people at the factory who built the car; thank you for the incredible new technology; thank you for the roads; thank you for the traffic signals to keep the roads safe; thank you for the street light; thank you for the trees; thank you for the birds I see flying by; thank you for all the homes for people to live in. The list goes on and on.

If you're in your room, say thank you for your bed; thank you for the dresser; thank you for your house; thank you for your closet; thank you for your clothes; thank you for the window in your room. Again, the list can include anything and everything.

PURPOSE OF THANK YOU MODE: There are two very important reasons why the *thank you* mode is a very valuable technique. First, you are giving thanks for most all the things you take for granted in this world. When you are thankful for what you have, you open the flood gates to receive even more. In addition, while you are being thankful, you are also being present of everything around you. As you do this, you'll come to realize how few times you've actually been present and paid attention to the world around you. Second, you have washed away all the negative thoughts that previously were occupying your mind. By flooding yourself with positive thoughts, it allows you to forget the original negative thoughts, and a *mind shift* can now take place.

After a *mind shift* occurs, you should say an affirmation that is focused on the goals you have. When your mind wanders again, and it will, just go back to the *thank you* mode until you have washed away the negative thoughts again. This may sound easy, and it is, but like anything else, it takes practice. Maybe at first it will take 15 minutes until you realize what's happened and then go into the *thank you* mode. With practice, you'll go down to ten minutes, then five minutes, and when you're really good, you'll start to catch negative thoughts right away.

Conversation Mind Shift

CONVERSATION MIND SHIFT: What if you are having a conversation with someone? Maybe the conversation starts off about homework, sports, or the upcoming weekend, and then it turns into gossip. It takes you about 15 minutes of gossiping about others until you've realized what's going on. Ego has crept in and taken control again. Of course, most likely the friend you're talking with has no knowl-edge of this *thinking stuff* and therefore is just acting *normal*. But you, the one who is trying to change your habits so you can take control of your life, realize what's just happened, yet you don't know how to reverse it. Do what I do. Immediately go into the thank you mode but pretend you are still engaged in the same conversation with your friend. Your friend will think you're listening, but in your mind you're saying thank for anything and everything you can see around you. This will help stop you from adding to the gossip. Smile while giving thanks and start turning the conversation in another direction. If your friend keeps pulling it back, just keep turning it elsewhere. If that doesn't work, it's time to go. Do not allow yourself to get trapped in someone else's negative vortex. Just as a black hole in space sucks in everything in its path, the negative conversation will do the same to you. So, if you can't change it, make up some reason for you to leave. Remember, all of this is in your control and sometimes you're going to have to make some hard choices. But it's your life, so take control of it, because if you don't, the outside world is going to.

Affirming What You Desire

AFFIRMATIONS: The word "affirm" means to declare something to be true. So when we use affirmations, the purpose is to convince our subconscious mind that what it is we want is actually already in our possession. The more we program ourselves to believe in already having or being something, the more likely it is to appear in our lives. Again, it matters not what you want. What does matter is how naturally you feel about having it in your physical possession at this moment. The following example is for an athlete envisioning his place on a team, but you can change it to fit whatever it is you want to focus on.

Example Affirmation

"Thank you for making the lacrosse team. It feels incredible to be on such a high-profile team. I love being a starter and contributing to the teams' success. It's great to have incredible camaraderie amongst all the players on the team. It's wonderful being the best player I can be and helping lead my team to victory. The energy flowing through my body as I score against the opponents is exhilarating. It's amazing how effortless it is for me to play at such a high level. I love the game of lacrosse, and it feels incredible to be such a high-performing player. Thank you, thank you, thank you."

The example above uses words carefully to inject a strong sense of feeling success along with the goal we have. The key is to *feel* the sensation of already being that player, so when we say the affirmation, we say it with strong feelings and in the present tense, as if we are already that player right now.

On the following lines, write down your own affirmation. Feel free to use the same sentences above, but change the goal to match your desire. Make it as long as you like. You should say your affirmation multiple times a day, especially when you first wake up, and just before falling asleep. As I mentioned throughout the book, when it starts to feel natural to you, the magic will begin to happen. You may have to read directly from your writing at first, but eventually you will have it memorized and will be able to say it throughout the day. It is your daily affirmations that help propel your thoughts in one direction.

Quotes

page 39   **"Difficult takes a day,
             impossible takes a week."**

                                    ➤ JAY Z

page 48   *"Faith is taking the first step when
             you don't see the whole staircase."*

                                    ➤ MARTIN LUTHER KING, JR.

page 58   *"Nothing is Impossible. The word
             itself says I'm Possible."*

                                    ➤ AUDREY HEPBURN

page 60   "Some things have to be
             believed to be seen."

                                    ➤ MADELEINE L'ENGLE

page 65   *"Be faithful in small things because it
             is in them that your strength lies."*

                                    ➤ MOTHER TERESA

page 74   "Holding onto anger is like
             drinking poison and expecting
             the other person to die."

                                    ➤ BUDDHA

page 78   "Just be yourself, there
             is no one better."

                                    ➤ TAYLOR SWIFT

Reading Sources

The Secret by Rhonda Byrne

Wishes Fulfilled by Dr. Wayne W. Dyer, Ph.D

The Power of Your Subconscious Mind by Joseph Murphy

The Power of Awareness by Neville

Think and Grow Rich by Napoleon Hill

Additional Reading Sources

The *Sara* books, 1, 2 & 3 by Esther and Jerry Hicks

The Law of Attraction by Esther and Jerry Hicks

The Magic, The Power & *Hero* by Rhonda Byrne

The Richest Man in Babylon by George S. Clason

The Alchemist by Paulo Coelho

The Art of Happiness by his Holiness the Dalai Lama and
Howard C. Cutler, M.D.

Peaks and Valleys by Spencer Johnson, M.D.

Dream Big I Dare You! Better Yet… I Double Dare You!! by
Roger Palmieri

The Four Agreements by Don Miguel Ruiz

Speaking Events

If you are interested in having the author, Todd J Courtney, speak at your school to engage the students, or speak at your company to guide the parents, on helping our youth move to a higher level, you can contact him at :

contact@teenscandream.com or

contact@thinkinginonedirection.com.

For many short e-books on multiple topics,
go to www.TeensCanDream.com

For inspirational nursery rhyme and children's books,
go to www.inpirationalnurseryrhymes.com

For kids struggling with leukemia and other cancers,
go to www.justimagineif.org

About the author,
go to www.toddjcourtney.com